Progress-Driven Entrepreneurs, Private Equity Finance and Regulatory Issues

Also by Zuhayr Mikdashi

FINANCIAL INTERMEDIATION IN THE 21st CENTURY

INTERNATIONAL BANKING: Innovations and New Policies

BANKERS' AND PUBLIC AUTHORITIES' MANAGEMENT OF RISKS

FINANCIAL STRATEGIES AND PUBLIC POLICIES: Banking, Insurance and Industry

TRANSNATIONAL OIL ISSUES: Policies and Perspectives

THE INTERNATIONAL POLITICS OF NATURAL RESOURCES

THE COMMUNITY OF OIL-EXPORTING COUNTRIES: A Study in Governmental Co-operation

CONTINUITY AND CHANGE IN THE WORLD OIL INDUSTRY

A FINANCIAL ANALYSIS OF MIDDLE EAST OIL CONCESSIONS: 1901–1965

REGULATING THE FINANCIAL SECTOR IN THE ERA OF GLOBALIZATION

Progress-Driven Entrepreneurs, Private Equity Finance and Regulatory Issues

Zuhayr Mikdashi
Professor Emeritus at the Faculty of Business and Economics, University of Lausanne, Switzerland

with

Chapter 6 by Benoit Leleux, *Stephan Schmidheiny Professor of Entrepreneurship and Finance at IMD, Switzerland*

Foreword by Samuel L. Hayes, *Jacob H. Schiff Professor of Investment Banking Emeritus at Harvard Business School, USA*

palgrave
macmillan

First published 2010 by
PALGRAVE MACMILLAN

Palgrave Macmillan in the UK is an imprint of Macmillan Publishers Limited, registered in England, company number 785998, of Houndmills, Basingstoke, Hampshire RG21 6XS.

Palgrave Macmillan in the US is a division of St Martin's Press LLC, 175 Fifth Avenue, New York, NY 10010.

Palgrave Macmillan is the global academic imprint of the above companies and has companies and representatives throughout the world.

Palgrave® and Macmillan® are registered trademarks in the United States, the United Kingdom, Europe and other countries

ISBN 978–0–230–51498–0

This book is printed on paper suitable for recycling and made from fully managed and sustained forest sources. Logging, pulping and manufacturing processes are expected to conform to the environmental regulations of the country of origin.

A catalogue record for this book is available from the British Library.

A catalog record for this book is available from the Library of Congress.

10 9 8 7 6 5 4 3 2 1
19 18 17 16 15 14 13 12 11 10

Printed and bound in Great Britain by
CPI Antony Rowe, Chippenham and Eastbourne

Contents

List of Exhibits and Boxes

Exhibits

Boxes

Foreword

Professor Mikdashi's new book on entrepreneurship via the private equity (PE) route is propitiously timed. As I write this, we are in the midst of the most serious economic turmoil since the Second World War. Most of the world's leading banks are suffering from large capital write-downs, and many have had to turn to their home governments for relief. This has sharply curbed their appetite for making loans, and many businesses are suffering from a lack of working capital financing, which is the lifeblood of commercial activity. Governments around the globe are trying hard to recharge their economies. They are also worrying about the longer-term underpinnings of their economies once the current liquidity crisis has abated. That concern for the longer-term sources of economic growth is where Professor Mikdashi's study of entrepreneurship comes to the fore.

It is a well-known element of the productivity equation that promoting innovation and creativity is essential to the long-run health of a national economy. And here we are not talking about the financial engineering 'innovations' that have brought the global economy to its current fragile state. Professor Mikdashi's focus is on the creation of new wealth via innovations in goods and services for which a current and future demand can be estimated. Often that process displaces vendors (and attendant jobs) of existing goods and services, which is painful to contemplate during a downturn, when many jobs are already being lost because of general shrinking demand. Over the longer term, the continued reinvention and renewal of a country's economic engine does involve a certain amount of creative destruction of existing plant and jobs, to make room for new or restructured business that will help an economy to continue to grow and create new jobs, greater capital investment and shareholder wealth. Professor Mikdashi's book is a study of the elements that are necessary to foster that reinvention process through the mobilization of investors to commit to private equity pools.

As Professor Mikdashi points out, there are alternative foci to the promotion of economic growth through private equity investment. One route is the birth of new businesses, but this 'new venture' track is typically the more risky one. Consumer acceptance of a new venture's product or service is uncertain, and the management team is usually untested. On the other hand, these start-ups can also be very efficient in stretching hard-to-get financial capital to its limits, and in wringing maximum effort from managers. Professor Mikdashi's study of the Grameen financing phenomenon in Bangladesh provides a good example of this. The talent and commercial drive of these (mainly women) entrepreneurs demonstrates just how powerful sweat equity can be when paired with a diminutive amount of capital. Other new ventures, however, rely on patient and deep-pocketed investors as a critical part of the equation. Professor Mikdashi's case study of an entrepreneur promoting innovation in the energy sector (he himself has extensive experience as an oil economist) suggests that there are many situations in which obtaining substantial (usually institutional) investors who can assure a venture's financial viability over a considerable period reduces the overall risk materially. Nonetheless, this large financial backing does not come without cost: the original principals in the ventures usually suffer a large dilution in their ownership stakes along the way. There are a number of private equity firms who have focused historically on venture capital investments. Professor Mikdashi discusses '3i' ('Investors in Industry') in Britain, which has done considerable venture capital investing. In the USA, Kleiner Perkins on the West Coast and Greylock Management on the East Coast have had consistently top quartile investment results.

Professor Mikdashi also discusses the entrepreneur's role in buying into already well-established businesses where management effectiveness has lagged and/or growth opportunities have been lost because of insufficient capital. This part of the private equity market is now much larger than the venture capital sector because it is less risky, offers the opportunity to employ debt leverage, and typically has a shorter time horizon from acquisition to investor exit. This sector has also played an important facilitating role in corporate restructuring in a number of countries, starting with the USA in the 1980s, then spreading – first to Europe and then, most recently, into Asia. Moreover, from the turn of the twenty-first century until the beginning of the financial meltdown in the second half of 2007, the returns earned by these 'leveraged buyouts (LBOs)' were more attractive than those earned from the new venture sector, which should have on average earned more because of the higher business risk.

While part of the reason for this superior performance was unusually generous credit available to the private equity firms, the LBO model has been sustained even in the face of the restricted debt levels existing since 2007. One can see why LBOs have persisted by thinking in terms of the three elements that determine the return on investment (ROI) for a private equity capital investor: (i) the efficiency with which assets can be turned over each year; (ii) the profit margins that can be earned on various of the firm's products and services; and (iii) the amount of borrowed funds that can be brought to minimize the investors' equity investment (this book discusses appropriate capital structures extensively). There are still many opportunities around the world to buy either privately-owned or publicly-traded businesses, rationalize their asset structures (for example, sell redundant assets, upgrade operating plant and equipment) and fine-tune their product or service lines (slimming down and focusing production and sales efforts on the highest-margin, least capital-intensive parts of the business). The fact that the third component of the profit equation (borrowed funds) is not as liberal as it once was does not necessarily have to drag down the investor's ROI. But it does require that the LBO firm pays less for the target company and/or improves margins and asset turnover sufficiently to offset the lower available leverage. And the prices of companies that have been purchased in the wake of the meltdown have indeed been significantly lower.

The book provides an in-depth primer on how the private equity firm uncovers candidate companies, investigates, values and negotiates an acquisition (PE firms try to avoid being pushed into an auction competition, pointing with pride to the proportion of their acquisitions where the arrangement was negotiated one-to-one, implying that the PE firm's involvement was worth more than just the highest price). Once the acquisition becomes a portfolio company, there is considerable discussion of how the PE firm works to increase the value of the company and ultimately manoeuvres to achieve a profitable exit, either through a strategic sale to another company (sometimes a competitor) or via a public offering of the stock.

There is a huge amount of private equity capital collected in pools as small as a few million dollars to some that are greater than US$13 billion. As the book points out, they have become important players in the financial markets and are much sought after as customers by merger-and-acquisition (M&A) intermediaries and (until recently) by commercial banks eager to handle their debt-financing business. Some observers have begun to wonder aloud about the ideal size for these investment pools. They have been expressing concern that the management companies of the largest funds can grow rich just by pocketing the annual 1 to 2 per cent fees without even considering the typical 20 per cent 'carry' that Professor Mikdashi points out has historically been the principal financial carrot to the LBO managers.

This book is rich in insights. It deserves a careful study!

SAMUEL L. HAYES
Cambridge, MA, USA
Harvard Business School

Preface

Distilling from past experiences, this book reflects on the actual or potential contributions of business leaders to progress. Progress is broadly defined here as sustainable advances over the long term in 'life satisfaction'. The latter is a composite of objective and subjective factors, measurable or imponderable – covering various aspects of human life. These include, *inter alia*, peace; justice and personal freedom; knowledge and education; trust and tolerance in social relations; effective control over corruption and crime; gainful employment; representative and effective government; innovation and creativity; socio-cultural accomplishments; and the preservation of the eco-system and bio-diversity.

From the general public-interest perspective, the ideal function of business leadership is to generate sustainable net benefits for a broad cross-section of stakeholders, thereby contributing to the progress of the widest possible circle of society's constituents. Relying on case studies of entrepreneurs and on empirical investigations of private equity executives, a blueprint for such progress-driven business leadership could conceivably be elaborated to guide key protagonists.

ZUHAYR MIKDASHI

Acknowledgements

Professor Samuel L. Hayes honours this book in the Foreword with his wise reflections based on a rich experience in academia and business, and in-depth scholarly research. He commands the respect of all those who have had the opportunity of listening to his addresses at Harvard Business School or in international venues. His books and articles in the field of finance have inspired academics, professionals, policy-makers and students worldwide. Imbued with humanism and universal values, he has been a trusted mentor to many.

I also welcome the outstanding original contribution of Professor Benoit Leleux in chapter 6 with his extensive research and professional experience in the subject matter of this book. His insightful analysis is bound to enrich our understanding of the dynamics of finance, notably that branch relating specifically to the private equity sector.

Professor Michel Antoine Habib (Professor of Finance at the University of Zürich's Swiss Banking Institute) and Dr Antoine Basile (economic adviser to international organizations) have kindly responded to my request for remarks on an early draft of this work (or parts of it). Their comments have been very helpful, and I express my gratitude for their time and effort.

Transforming a manuscript into a book requires several dedicated and high quality skills within publishing quarters. In this respect, the author is particularly obliged to Lisa von Fircks (Senior Commissioning Editor – Finance, at Palgrave Macmillan) for advice, and to Keith Povey and his colleagues for copy-editing and the index. Their expertise, their painstaking efforts, and their courtesies toward the author are hereby gratefully recognized.

Finally, I would be remiss not to mention my family's empathy. I remain solely responsible for the content of my work.

ZUHAYR MIKDASHI

Notes on the Contributors

Zuhayr Mikdashi is Professor Emeritus at the University of Lausanne, Switzerland, Faculty of Business and Economics. He is the Founding Director of the Institute of Banking and Financial Management (later shortened to Institute of Banking and Finance) at the University of Lausanne, Switzerland. Professor Mikdashi was previously Tenured Professor of Business Administration at the American University of Beirut, Lebanon; on the Visiting Faculty at the Graduate School of Business, University of Indiana, Bloomington, USA; Research Fellow at the Center for International Affairs, Harvard University, USA. He was previously Research Fellow at the Japanese Institute for Developing Economies, Tokyo, Japan and Visiting Fellow at the foundation 'Resources for the Future', Washington, DC, USA. He has also been guest speaker at several academic colloquia; organizer of international symposia for business leaders, regulators, and academics; adviser or consultant (for the World Bank, UN agencies, OPEC, OECD Development Centre, Arab Monetary Fund, and various national or trans-national institutions); Resident Adviser to the Minister of Finance and Oil, State of Kuwait; Adviser, World Economic Forum, Geneva. He is the author or co-author of books and articles on finance, socio-economic development, and the political economy of natural resources. His previous book is *Regulating the Financial Sector in the Era of Globalization* (Palgrave Macmillan, 2003).

Samuel L. Hayes holds the Jacob H. Schiff Chair in Investment Banking Emeritus, at the Harvard Business School, USA. He has taught at the School since 1970, prior to which he was a tenured member of the faculty of the Columbia University Graduate School of Business. His MBA teaching assignments have included the second-year courses in Investment Banking, Management of Financial Services Organizations, and Corporate Financial Management, as well as the first-year Finance course (where he served as Course Head). For eight years he served as head of the Analytics Program for entering MBAs. He has also chaired Harvard's International Senior Managers Program in Vevey, Switzerland. He taught in the summer Corporate Financial

Management Program for senior finance executives for a number of years and chaired that faculty during six of those years. He has taught in HBS Executive Education's Advanced Management Program and Owner-President Management Program. He founded the executive education program Strategic Finance for Smaller Businesses and chaired that program for the past fourteen years. He also headed and taught the International Senior Manager Program from 1979–1981. Professor Hayes' research has focused on the capital markets and on the corporate interface with the securities markets. He has written numerous working papers and articles on related topics in journals such as the *Harvard Business Review*, the *Accounting Review*, the *Financial Analysis Journal, The Economic Review*, and *Financial Management*, and has contributed chapters to a number of books. Two articles which he co-authored on real estate finance won the Shattuck Award for the best article on real estate in 1967 and 1972. Professor Hayes is the co-author or editor of seven books, including *Competition in the Investment Banking Industry* (Harvard University Press, 1983), *Investment Banking and Diligence* (Harvard Business School Press, 1986), *Wall Street and Regulation* (Harvard Business School Press, 1987), *Investment Banking: A Tale of Three Cities* (Harvard Business School Press, 1990), *Managing Financial Institutions* (The Dryden Press/HBJ, 1992), *Financial Services: Perspectives and Challenges* (Harvard Business School Press, 1993), and *Islamic Law and Finance: Religion, Risk, and Return* (Kluwer Press, 1997). Professor Hayes has consulted for a number of corporations, financial institutions, and government agencies, including the Justice Department, the Treasury Department, the Federal Trade Commission, and the Securities and Exchange Commission, where he served on the Tully Commission in 1994–1995 to examine compensation arrangements for stock brokers. For twelve years, he was Chairman of the Finance Advisory Board of the Commonwealth of Massachusetts. He currently serves on the Board of Managers of Swarthmore College (where he is Chair of the Investment Committee) and the Board of Trustees of the New England Conservatory of Music. He served for more than twenty years on the Boards of the Eaton-Vance family of mutual funds (where he was Chairman) and Tiffany & Company. He currently serves on the boards of Telect, Inc., and Yakama, Inc. and is on the advisory boards of Edward Jones and Arcapita, Inc.

Benoit Leleux is the Stephan Schmidheiny Professor of Entrepreneurship and Finance at IMD, Switzerland. He also directs the CEO Seminars and the MBA Startup Projects. Professor Leleux was previously Visiting Professor of Entrepreneurship at INSEAD and Director of the 3i VentureLab and Associate Professor and Zubillaga Chair in Finance and Entrepreneurship at Babson College, Wellesley, MA (USA) from 1994 to 1999. He obtained his PhD at INSEAD, specializing in Corporate Finance and Venture Capital. Benoît Leleux is a specialist in venture financing and management, combining expertise in entrepreneurship, venture capital, private equity and growth management. His experience includes four years of corporate venturing in South East Asia for a major agribusiness conglomerate. He is active in a number of private equity funds, as well as numerous startup companies in Europe and the US, either as director, investor, and/or advisor. Recent research papers look at emerging market venture capital business models and the private equity investment profiles of family offices. He authored a number of books, including *From Microfinance to Small Business Finance: The Business Case for Private Capital Investments* (Palgrave Macmillan, 2007), *Nurturing Science-Based Startups: An International Case Perspective* (Springer Verlag, 2007) and *A European Casebook on Entrepreneurship and New Ventures* (Prentice-Hall, 1996). His works earned some distinguished awards, including the 1996 Best Paper Award in International Finance at the FMA conference in New York and the 1996 Best Paper Award at the Academy of Entrepreneurial Finance. His teaching cases have repeatedly won both EFMD European Case Writing Awards and ECCH European Case Awards.

Part 1
Entrepreneurs Overcoming Challenges

Successful entrepreneurs are often viewed as socio-economic heroes whenever they create lasting values for society. These entrepreneurs' achievements cannot be evaluated properly unless their activities are placed in their proper context. The case studies analyzed in Part 1 attempt to present succinctly relevant aspects of the social and economic environment of the entrepreneurs concerned; and to identify local, regional or global challenges they have encountered. In anchoring achievements in their setting, one can better visualize the entrepreneurs' projects, comprehend their efforts, and appreciate the results obtained. Furthermore, the analysis attempts to evaluate the significance of business size, stakeholders-wide performance and market dynamics for entrepreneurial activities.

1
Case Studies

In searching for the identification of entrepreneurial characteristics as they relate to progress, three inspiring case studies are presented here, and evaluated within their historical and socio-economic context. They are drawn from both developed and developing countries across three continents – America, Asia and Africa. The cited entrepreneurs are chosen for their roles as engines or accelerators of 'net value creation' for the benefit of their stakeholders. The latter comprise, in particular, those who have a legitimate interest in the success of the business – notably employees, investors, various business partners, the surrounding community, and the local or national authorities. Stakeholders' interests cover, *inter alia*, the pursuit of business profitability, balanced sharing in benefits, and societal progress.

The activities of the three chosen entrepreneurs are in widely different sectors: *industrial–technological* (power generation); *services* (microfinance); and *consumer goods* (artisans'/artists' products). Nevertheless, they illustrate role models of success worthy of emulation, all thriving on a culture of competition aimed at creating genuine value for their stakeholders, and opening up new opportunities for society to progress. The first profiled entrepreneur Stanford R. Ovshinsky, a Lithuanian immigrant to the United States, searches for *sustainable* 'clean energy technologies'. The second entrepreneur Muhammad Yunus, from Bangladesh, seeks to empower the poor and the marginalized with microfinance. The third entrepreneur Serigne Babacar Mbow, from Senegal, endeavours to rejuvenate his community via a hub of 'tradition-inspired art and craftsmanship' underpinned by 'work ethos'.

The first case of entrepreneurship is drawn from the world's largest and technologically most advanced economy in the first decade of the twenty-first century, namely the United States. The case concerns an entrepreneur who seeks the development of new technologies for *clean, renewable, readily accessible, widely available, affordable* and *safe* sources energy. By having the foregoing six attributes, such sources of energy become perennially sustainable. Compared to the currently dominant hydrocarbon fuels (coal, oil, natural gas), solar and hydrogen energies come close to satisfying the above-mentioned criteria – apart from *affordability*. They protect planet Earth from the greenhouse or noxious gases generated from hydrocarbons and other sources, mainly in the form of carbon dioxide (CO_2), followed by methane (CH_4), nitrous oxide (N_2O), hydrofluorcarbons (HFCs), perfluorcarbons (PFCs), and sulphur hexafluoride (SF_6) (Deutsch, 2008).

The two other cases of entrepreneurs presented below are particularly interesting in so far as they are drawn from two of the world's poorest developing countries that suffer from dysfunctional deficient socio-economic institutions, limited material resources, high endemic unemployment, and a deteriorating ecological environment. These two entrepreneurs' success is particularly edifying in view of colossal chronic difficulties generally encountered in their poor and heavily indebted home countries, namely:

- Bangladesh in South Asia, which is regularly hit by deadly cyclones that kill thousands of farmers and fishermen (flattening or sweeping away their dwellings, which consist mainly of tin sheds), destroying property, crops and domestic animals, and leading to the devastating encroachment of the sea over arable land. On average, some 40 per cent of Bangladesh's land area is flooded annually – affecting an estimated half of its population of some 150 million living crowded together precariously almost at sea level. These regular disasters render famine and diseases endemic.
- Senegal in West Africa, which is drought-exposed and faced with the calamitous situation of desertification (another effect of climate change). A large proportion of its population is jobless and lives in destitute conditions with bleak prospects. These people are thus driven to leave their homes in search of a livelihood abroad. They do so in dangerous conditions, and often at the risk of their lives.

Entrepreneurs from poorer countries (here Bangladesh and Senegal) have achieved praiseworthy results, despite the fact that they operate in typically underdeveloped economies with multiple handicaps. Indeed, they lack – unlike entrepreneurs from advanced economies – ready access to efficient infrastructures (such as schools and hospitals, transportation, telecommunications, energy, drinking water and waste management), efficient financial intermediaries, appropriate legal–institutional frameworks, attractive governmental incentives or stimuli, sound macroeconomic policies that favour entrepreneurship, and/or effective rescue-aid programmes to reach those struck by disaster.

The 'general' and the 'sector-specific' socio-economic context encountered by each entrepreneur are presented succinctly to place their activities in a proper perspective. Indeed, such background information serves to describe the challenges encountered by the studied entrepreneurs, and to judge their personal efforts as catalysts of change and energizers of hitherto untapped reservoirs of creativity, overcoming a variety of difficulties in imaginative ways to realize their innovative projects.

Case A: Sustainable energy technologies

The energy conundrum

To understand the laborious entrepreneurial efforts of Ovshinsky in accomplishing his innovative projects, one needs to comprehend the challenges encountered by human beings in the vital domain of energy. Such information should allow a better understanding of the ambitions of the entrepreneur concerned in spending several decades of his life attempting to translate his vision of a clean and abundant source of energy into a workable reality for the benefit of all human beings, wherever they are.

Functions of energy, and demand–supply issues

Major leaps in human progress have been facilitated by successive developments of *material* energy to replace or complement the *muscular* energy exerted by humans and/or their domesticated animals. The development of non-muscular energy has been spectacular since the eighteenth century. Outstanding scientific–technological innovations in the energy field have permitted the harnessing of nature's forces and resources into heating or cooling, light, transport, communication, mechanical work, pressure, or catalytic transformations. Nevertheless, certain energy sources generate important negative externalities at various stages – from production to transport, transformation, storage, and usage. These include waste; harmful emissions affecting health, nature and climate; and competition with other basic human needs (mainly food).

An economy's optimal 'energy mix' should satisfy over the long term, and as well as possible, several basic criteria. These are:

(a) energy efficiency (that is, the capacity to generate for an end use – say, a given amount of lighting for a standard room – an energy *output* in excess of the energy *input* needed to generate that said output;
(b) economic efficiency (that is, the capacity to create significant net value, over and above the cost of all inputs used);
(c) respect for the environment;
(d) perennial abundance;
(e) reliable, widely accessible and decentralized supplies;
(f) affordable;
(g) easy to store or use;
(h) least susceptible to grave accidents which could impact irreversibly the quality of life on planet Earth, and
(i) not pre-empting other vital human needs (such as food).

On the demand side, consumers and users as well as manufacturers of energy-using equipment or tools should strive to contain demand for energy through multi-track approaches. Among these is the use of energy-efficient equipment (along the whole chain covering the production, transport, transformation, storage, and use of energy). Minimization of waste (as much as 80 per cent is lost in the energy chain) is crucial. Moreover, best practices in energy conservation also call for judicious policies and planning in a variety of fields: appropriate urban and regional zoning; optimal logistics to reduce the superfluous movement of people and/or products; suitable designs for buildings (to minimize the energy consumption for heat or cooling, ventilation, and light); the use of insulating construction materials, thus avoiding energy wastage; the means and frequency of public transport; the choice of methods of production; and other related policies.

Energy mix and social costs

While suppliers and users of fossil fuels have shown some interest in alternative sources of clean and renewable energy (solar, geothermal, biomass, wind, hydrogen, tidal, for example), their relatively limited investments in these sources can largely be explained by: (a) their huge accumulated investments and know-how in the production and use of fossil fuels and their derivatives; and (b) the heavy investments required over several years to make clean and renewable alternatives commercially competitive. Providers and users of fossil fuels have, indeed, a guarded position *vis-à-vis* 'revolutionary technological innovations', lest the latter's competition threatens the performance of their current core activities. For example, vehicle manufacturers (along with their customers and subcontractors) have so far balked at writing-off their huge investments in the usage of fossil fuels pending technological breakthroughs in alternative clean energy supported by adequate financial–fiscal incentives and a strong public opinion.

The public authorities' support for clean energy should at least match the social cost of pollution generated by the established commercial sources of energy (such as coal or oil). Indeed, authorities in many countries – under the strong influence of public opinion – have become keen on moderating or reducing the consumption of fossil fuels (hard coal, lignite/brown coal, petroleum) because of their collateral damage. Such damage shows up mostly in the form of carbon dioxide (CO_2) emissions with a 'greenhouse effect' on the climate, as well as in oil spills resulting from accidents or the unauthorized cleaning of vessels' fuel tanks, in violation of international maritime law (and causing destruction to fauna and flora, damaging fishing and tourism, and putting people's health or lives in danger). The warming of the Earth's climate is generally considered a serious threat to the environment, exacerbating desertification and weather turbulence such as flooding. It can collaterally open-up certain previously frozen regions to economic exploitation – for example, land cultivation and mineral extraction closer to the Arctic Circle. Nevertheless, the consensus among researchers is that damage from CO_2 gas emissions (unless neutralized through investment in appropriate technology) far outweighs any eventual benefits. This has been substantiated by the Intergovernmental Panel on Climate Change (IPCC) (see UN Conference on Climate Change, 2007; and OECD, 2008).

One should point out that renewable sources of energy are not invariably environmentally friendly or socially desirable. Thus large hydroelectric dams built in tropical areas such as Brazil are also a source of methane gas (produced from vegetation accumulating at the bottom of water reservoirs, where there is little or no oxygen) with environmentally harmful greenhouse effects. Reportedly, methane has a more negative effect on climate change than an equivalent power station burning fossil fuels – but it has been suggested that the methane from hydro-electric dams can be exploited to produce electricity (see Hirsch, 2007, citing the National Institute for Space Research, which monitors the Amazon Rainforest: see www.inpe.br). The damming of rivers has undeniable advantages in generating electricity, regulating water flows, allowing for the irrigation of arid land and so on. Nevertheless, they also have potential drawbacks which vary from one geographical area to another and include: the retention of certain sediments that would otherwise have fertilized arable land downstream of the dam; the burying of ancient vestiges of the past; the displacement of large communities; the erosion of the river's shores that causes landslides; a deterioration in the quality of water; destruction of aquatic life; and adverse climatic changes, among others. The following drawbacks apply, *inter alia*, to the world's largest dam system – the Three Gorges Dam that spans the Yangtse River in China (see, for example, Macartney, 2007).

Energy versus food

Agrofuels (a term describing the whole range of energy products extracted from agricultural sources) are presented by interested quarters as being less harmful to the environment, compared to hydrocarbons. Yet their production is not without drawbacks for society, as explained below.

Agrofuels cover *ethanol* and *biodiesel*. Ethanol can be produced from cereals, sugar cane, sugar beet, potatoes, wood cellulose and other biomass. Biodiesel is derived from palm oil, rapeseed and wood. Devoting scarce arable land on Planet Earth (in the absence of fallow areas) to the production of agrofuels has potentially negative effects in so far as:

(a) it is made at the expense of food production – hurting in particular the poor (whose income is principally spent on food) through shortages and higher prices;

(b) it leads to the clearance of forests in order to grow cereals for agrofuel, despite it being known that forests are essential for the absorption of CO_2;
(c) it could require more 'energy input' than that produced in 'energy output' assessed over the whole 'energy chain', from the initial stage of production until the ultimate use by consumers;
(d) it is a big user of soft water and of hydrocarbons-based fertilizer with polluting drawbacks; and
(e) it is less sustainable than other clean, renewable sources of energy (see OECD, 2007; *The Economist*, 2007a).

Another drawback of ethanol is that the nitrogen- and phosphorus-based fertilizers used to grow maize in the US Midwest for the production of ethanol are fatal to sea life. These fertilizers reach the Gulf of Mexico through the Mississippi and Atchafalaya rivers, deplete the sea's oxygen through algal growth, and suffocate life in the bottom and near-bottom waters (thereby damaging the valuable Gulf fishery sector). It is thus reckoned that an area off the states of Louisiana and Texas, and larger in size than the state of New Jersey (7,900 square miles or 20,500 square kilometres), known as the Dead Zone, is affected by this problem (see National Oceanic and Atmospheric Administration, *NOAA Magazine*, item 2669: www.noaanews.noaa.gov; also *Bloomberg Markets*, 2007).

The need for a holistic, longer-term policy

Market prices (inclusive of taxes) of current sources of energy have not so far taken fully into account the actual or potential *drawbacks* of using each source of energy over the longer term. Drawbacks cover four categories of factors:

(a) the negative externalities of each of the major sources of energy (coal, oil, gas and nuclear) that have an adverse effect on human health and the Earth's environment;
(b) the exhaustible nature of these fuels (this applies to hydrocarbons, as well as to uranium ore used in the generation of atomic/nuclear power);
(c) risks linked to rumours, misinformation and/or speculation, which generate price volatility; and
(d) geopolitical uncertainties with respect to the security of supplies.

The above-mentioned costs and risks (both physical and political) should be reasonably estimated and 'interiorized' in the pricing of various sources of energy at the production, transport, transformation, storage, distribution and use levels. Cost estimates should comprise the pollution of land, water, soil or air in the course of operation or for reasons of recklessness and accidents. They should also include the risk of potential disruption of supplies.

The principles of 'polluter–payer' and of 'waster–payer' have been increasingly clamoured for by the general public, and adopted in the legislative corpus of advanced economies. Objective and measurable standards of actual and potential damages need to be established to implement the foregoing principles. Such measurements should help in obtaining a more comprehensive picture of the relative attractiveness of various sources of energy in order to devise an optimal policy of energy mix.

Governments in ecologically-minded societies have thus tended increasingly to impose anti-pollution regulations on energy producers, transporters, refiners, distributors, and/or ultimate users. These cover the responsibility of purifying fuels before their use, the commitment to return affected energy-producing sites (with their flora and fauna) to a situation approximating to their initial pre-exploitation condition, or the payment of appropriate charges to defray relevant estimated damages sustained by society. Public opinion in certain countries have forced their authorities effectively to bar certain energy sources: this applies, for example, to nuclear power, fearing for grave accidents resulting from human error, maleficent acts or natural disasters (such as earthquakes), and knowing that nuclear waste (from the mining stage of uranium often carried out in the open, up to the decommissioning of power plants) remains radioactive – with risks of contaminating soil, water and air, possibly for several generations or centuries. Governmental interdictions in some countries also apply to logging, fearing this will result in desertification or climate change.

Through fiscal, financial, administrative measures and sanctions, public authorities can obtain for their economy the desired energy mix. Viewed over the long term, hydrogen–solar fuels meet the clean energy criteria, along with hydropower, wind power or biomass. Yet, more technological toil and industrial investments need to be committed, in order to improve the economic yield (net value added), and the energy efficiency (excess of energy output over energy input) to enhance the economic attractiveness and competitiveness of hydrogen–solar energy. Nevertheless, such desirable sources of energy would have to compete with a variety of vested interests in international markets currently dominated by long-established powerful enterprises that have been investing heavily in producing and commercializing 'fossil fuels'.

Exhaustive studies are still needed, to examine and assess the positive and negative impacts at each stage of the 'supply chain' of each source of energy – whether currently available or under development. Changes are bound to be slow over the short term, in view of (a) the information needed for policy choices and their implementation; (b) the sluggish responsiveness of supply/demand patterns to governmental actions and market variables (notably prices); and (c) the long gestation periods needed for research and technological innovation to come to fruition. As it takes several years to build or develop commerical energy supplies (such as hydro-electric dams, nuclear power plants and hydrocarbon deposits), delaying investment in periods of low or moderate energy prices could presage a future era of shortage of energy supplies with higher prices.

Analysts cannot neglect the impact of socio-political–military actions on the supply–demand equation. It is reasonable to assume that the disruption of oil supplies has been a major cause of price increases. These disruptions have resulted from the destruction of oil facilities (for example, in Iraq over the period 1990–2008); the embargo imposed by advanced economies on the development of hydrocarbon fields in oil-producing countries deemed to be unfriendly (USA versus Iran in the first decade of the twenty-first century); and the endemic civil strife of disgruntled indigenous communities *vis-à-vis* their national authorities (in the oil-rich Niger delta), – to mention just a few cases.

A pragmatic visionary

Challenges exposed above regarding harnessing energy for human progress have been the driving force behind Stanford Ovshinsky's inventions and entrepreneurial activities. Helped by his wife Iris, he focussed on solar power and hydrogen seeking to meet as closely as possible the following criteria: safe, environmentally friendly, maintenance-free, renewable, reasonably easy to handle, affordable, and with decentralized availability (see *The Economist Technology Quarterly*, 2006, 2008; also 'Inventor of the Week Archive' – Stanford Ovshinsky', Lemelson–MIT Program: http://web.mit.edu/invent/iow/ovshinsky.html).

Stanford Ovshinsky's life and achievements show him to be an autodidact scientist, a prolific inventor, and an industrial entrepreneur with a clear vision of human progress. In focusing on the energy sector, his primary concern has been to address directly a vital societal problem – namely, the energy/environmental crisis of the twenty-first century – of prime concern to humankind. Rivalry for the control of scarce supplies of commercial energy can, indeed, be a potential source of conflict, and may lead to war among governments seeking to control energy resources that are concentrated in certain geographical regions. Guided by the family motto 'With the oppressed, against the oppressor', inspired by the peace and civil-rights movements, Stanford Ovshinsky and his wife share the humanist values and ideals of the other entrepreneurs (Mbow and Yunus) profiled below.

Among Ovshinsky's entrepreneurial characteristics, a few are especially notable. They include the following features:

1 *Self-taught*: doing odd jobs during the day to support his family during the Great Depression, he attended a technical night school to learn how to run a machine shop. With no possibility of accessing a college education to satisfy his enthusiasm for science and technology because of his poverty, he studied on his own in the public libraries of his home town of Akron, Ohio, driven by an insatiable curiosity for learning.
2 *Prolificacy*: Ovshinsky's creativity can be judged by the number of his patents (close to 400 by 2009) that have been used. He was relentless in his scientific–technological pursuits despite a dearth of funds and adverse economic circumstances.
3 *Visionary and pragmatic*: his innovations represent a capacity to combine intellectual modelling with the practicality of an engineer. Modestly, he acknowledges that his achievements could not have been accomplished without the vital contributions of talented colleagues and collaborators.
4 *Unwavering in his core mission* of long-term progress aimed at developing and harnessing clean, perennially abundant, widely

available and readily usable sources of energy (such as hydrogen gas or liquid derived from the sea water that covers three-quarters of the Earth's surface, and/or the sun whose incandescence derives from burning hydrogen) to become affordable enough to replace polluting fossil hydrocarbon fuels, which are subject to rapid depletion.

5 *His enthusiasm* combined with friendliness has enabled him to mobilize eminent inventors and other experts from industry or academia to advise him or work on his projects within a non-hierarchical team of collaborators. His multiculturalism and compassion for the excluded have proved to be crucial in attracting talents from among minorities.

6 *Momentum maintained at an advanced age*: his entrepreneurial spirit has never wavered throughout his long life, maintaining his achievements in tandem with his biochemist wife and partner for some fifty years Iris Miroy Dibner. Sadly, Iris died suddenly while swimming in 2006 at the age of 79. Ovshinsky retired from their company Energy Conversion Devices Inc. (ECD) shortly afterwards and launched a new company in 2007 – Ovshinsky Innovation LLC – in partnership with a physicist, Dr Rosa Chiang Young, who had been his collaborator for over 23 years at ECD and who became his wife in 2007. At the age of 86 (at the time of writing), he is recognized as still being full of inventiveness (see 'Inventor Reinvents Himself: Battery, Solar Pioneer Strikes Out on Own', and 'Stan Ovshinsky: Inventor Is Still Full of Energy', *The Detroit News*, 4 December 2007 and 31 May 2008, respectively, www.detnews.com; and Avery Cohn, 'A Revolution Fuelled by the Sun', *Berkeley Review of Latin American Studies*, University of California at Berkeley, Spring 2008, pp. 22–7; and 'Stanford R. Ovshinsky', 18 January 2009, http://en.wikipedia.org).

Ovshinsky described how he began his business thus:

My wife [Iris] and I formed the company (ECD) on January 1, 1960. We wanted to use science and technology to solve the world's serious social problems. We decided to focus our efforts on energy, in hopes of achieving 'the ultimate' – by that I mean using hydrogen and the sun as the energy source. We wanted to begin the process of decoupling energy from fossil fuels. (*The Ultimate Global*

Citizen – An Interview with Stanford Ovshinsky, CEO of Energy Conversion Devices, interviewer Allen Flickinger, MBA2, 5 March 2001: rflickin@umich.edu)

Among his many inventions in the energy field, his most important contributions have been in two major areas:

(a) Thin-film flexible photovoltaic (PV) solar panels which generate electricity, and the machines to produce them. The panels are characterized by their flexibility, durability, light weight and ease of installation. This branch has proved commercially profitable in recent years, in view of the surge in the price of hydrocarbons.
(b) Nickel-metal-hydride (NiMH) batteries. These are powerful batteries usable in electrically-powered vehicles or in hybrid-powered vehicles with dual engines using fuel (such as petrol) and electrically-powered motors. A solid hydride is a sponge-like material of alloys with a disordered structure that can absorb hydrogen gas (instead of storing it at high pressure), thus making it convenient, safe, and easy to store and transport at ambient pressure.

In August 2005, ECD unveiled a Toyota Prius vehicle with an internal combustion engine powered entirely by pollution-free hydrogen supplied from solid-state hydrogen storage cylinders and using NiMH batteries. The batteries convert hydrogen directly into electricity, which feeds an electric motor (see Kridel, 2006). In operation, hydrogen combines with oxygen to discharge water. Therefore the burning of hydrogen does not have any disadvantages apart from the production of humidity, which may be inconvenient. Hydrogen is a material available in great abundance on Earth – in a wide spectrum of combinations, such as water, whose chemical composition is H_2O (as well as in combination with carbon, in the form of hydrocarbons). Much energy is needed to split water atoms into hydrogen and oxygen, and ideally solar energy from PV can be used to power the electrolyte machines capable of doing the splitting. However, the major challenge is to store the hydrogen gas, and this has been made possible by the NiMH technology (see www.ovonic.com).

In comparison with serveral competitors developing solar-electric panel technologies, Ovshinsky's thin-film PV products are lighter, more durable, and cheaper to produce (owing to large-scale production and lesser use of silicon). Moreover, his products are more flexible (being readily adaptable to a variety of surfaces), more efficient in capturing low ambient light (for example, on a rainy day), and readily usable in a variety of domains – notably as direct roofing material in homes, office buildings or factories.

Professional collective organizations, industrial firms and venture capitalists have sunk substantial funds into Ovshinsky's company (ECD) or its affiliates, such as ECD Ovonics. Industrial groups have been mainly corporate energy suppliers or users: Atlantic Richfield Oil Corp., Standard Oil of Ohio (later both acquired by BP), Canon, Bekaert NV, General Motors (GM), and Texaco (which merged later with Chevron). Texaco's funding exceeded US$150 million (see www.cobasys.com/news/PressReleases/20010718.htm), GM's funding amounted to US$20 million, and the U.S. Advanced Battery Consortium's grants amounted to US$36 million (see *Time* magazine, 1 March 1999; available at: www.time.com/time/reports/environment/heroes). The total estimated funding of ECD reached half a billion dollars over forty years before any profit was generated (see US Securities and Exchange Commission, Energy Conversion Devices, Inc., 2007). The funding was made by industrial corporations acting as venture capitalists. In view of their limited time horizon, during which their expectations of rapid breakthroughs and benefits did not materialize, they resorted to writing off the bulk of their investments in ECD.

Ovshinsky's leading commercial success has been in harnessing inexhaustible solar energy through photovoltaic (PV) materials that convert sunlight into electricity. The demand for PV products has soared since around 2005, as consumers have become concerned about energy shortages, the depletion of finite fossil resources, rising or volatile prices of hydrocarbons, and the environmental problems mentioned above (see, for example, Fialka, 2006).

Ovshinsky's innovations, one can conclude, have the merit of being founded on perennial progress that is respectful of the environment. The *pay-off* may well extend over a time horizon of several decades, as has generally been the case with the introduction of novel energy technologies. The profitable commercialization of such innovations is a long and gradual process, and will materialize subject to the cumulative impact of additional innovations and experiments by several inventors-cum-entrepreneurs aimed at technical improvements; sizeable production and distribution facilities that can take advantage of economies of scale and appropriate financial–fiscal incentives provided by the public authorities (see also Academic Network in Entrepreneurship, Innovation and Finance; available at: www.gate2growth.com).

Case B: Lending to the enterprising poor

Similar to entrepreneurship in the domain of energy, entrepreneurship in the domain of finance can best be understood by examining the relevant background information. The case study analysed below shows that poverty is not an unalterable condition that shackles creativity and value-creation and progress. Poor people can overcome, as illustrated hereafter.

Bankable individuals

Some 2 billion of the world's total population (estimated at about 6.5 billion at the beginning of the twenty-first century) live on less than US$2 a day, and more than 1 billion live on US$1 a day. In the absence of sufficient assets or a sound financial history, the poor have thus often been left to the mercy of abusers, such as usurers charging exorbitant exploitative interest rates.

Conventional commercial banks have generally shunned the poor (those without sufficient collateral to offer as security for a loan), and have focused on the middle and upper classes of society in view of the guarantees offered by their assets or income. Mainstream commercial financial institutions typically require the security of assets or evidence of a steady income before extending credit. The material collateral requirement (which may be realized if the borrower defaults) is, however, no guarantee of the solvency of loans – in so far as the value of such collateral could be overestimated or could tumble following market vagaries or slumps. Behaviour characterized by prudent borrowing, productive investment, rigour in monitoring, avoidance of profligacy, prompt repayment of obligations, and solidarity among poor borrowers can prove to be the equivalent of a 'bankable asset'. Such behaviour offers lenders less of a risk, compared to collateralized loans to non-creditworthy borrowers.

As conceived and developed by business and social leaders, microfinance is intended as one among several means enabling the hitherto excluded segments of society to access finance for productive activities (as opposed to consumption). The poor and low-income segments of society, with no assets to offer as collateral for their borrowing, have the capacity to honour financial obligations, thanks to sustainable income-generating activities and discipline.

Since the 1980s, microfinance institutions have become economically viable, and have shown that, as a result of responsible lending, poverty is not an inescapable fate. Indeed, microfinance beneficiaries have the potential to become entrepreneurial, self-reliant and productive. Microfinance institutions that provide the poor with basic financial services operate on the principle that the debtor's *character* (notably his/her prudence, rigour and hard work) is superior in credit value to *material collateral*. Experience has confirmed to these institutions the validity of this principle that enables lenders to recoup their non-collateralized loans.

The concept of financing the underdogs and the hungry by non-governmental institutions has been espoused by several social scientists and development activists: among these in modern times, a name often mentioned is that of Akhtar Hameed Khan (1914–99), who worked in this field in various countries – notably in India, Pakistan and Bangladesh. In these countries, and others in South Asia, significant segments of society suffer from debt bondage (akin to financial slavery) in so far as parents and children are attached permanently to landlords or business potentates in order to service their debts: they work in fields, quarries, construction sites, textile looms, and in other sweatshops or hazardous activities for insufficient pay to reimburse debts. The majority of these debts were originally incurred by hapless people for emergency expenses (medical bills, food, the funeral of a relative, for example), dowries, religious ceremonies, housing, or vices such as drinking or gambling (see, for example, Srivastava, 2005; Daru *et al.*, 2003).

Microfinance has expanded considerably since the early 1970s in Bangladesh, after the country's secession from Pakistan and its independence in 1971. Major projects started in the 1970s include: (1) a programme to lend to the poor pioneered in 1974 by Muhammad Yunus; (2) the non-governmental organization Bangladesh Rural Advancement Committee (BRAC), established in 1972 by Fazle Hasan

Abed to alleviate poverty and empower the poor across the whole country, providing microcredit since 1979; and (3) the Association for Social Advancement (ASA), founded by Shafiqual Haque Choudhury, whose microcredit programme began in 1991 (see www.grameen-info.org; www.brac.net; www.asabd.org).

The foremost internationally recognized developer of microfinance, Muhammad Yunus, began his work in 1974, a year of famine in his home country, Bangladesh, where he was a professor of economics at the University of Chittagong. His first concrete measure was to lend directly from his personal savings to a group of forty-two women in a village in southern Bangladesh (Jobra) a sum equivalent to US$27, to finance their business of bamboo furniture. This was followed by other loans guaranteed by Yunus from local banks. Such an approach had limitations, which led Yunus to embark on the entrepreneurial launch of the Grameen (*meaning village in Bengali*) Bank in 1983. Grameen has thus set up an edifying model for a worldwide movement of lending modest sums to the poor and low-income individuals, who were hitherto excluded from conventional bank lending, to help support their self-employment.

Grameen Bank also encourages its customers to deposit their savings – no matter how small – instead of hoarding their money, as had been the case traditionally in view of the reluctance of conventional commercial banks to accept small sums on deposit. Grameen Bank furthermore offers its customers services for transfers/settlements, pension funds, insurance products, financial literacy courses, business training and counselling, cellular phoning (providing networking opportunities for hitherto isolated individuals and communities), investment funds (invested in joint ventures with international companies in such business sectors as food, potable water, telecommunications, energy, textiles, among others).

Bangladesh ranks among the poorest countries in the world, and is notoriously exposed to natural calamities, as mentioned earlier (notably devastating recurrent tropical storms and inundations, famine and disease). The aim of Yunus and his like has been to help a large number of people to move from a state of destitution to one of dignified living, with ultimately positive effects on society at large. The vast majority of beneficiaries have been women (traditionally disfavoured by men's ascendancy) seeking very small loans (generally around US$100 per borrower) to establish or expand small, self-sustaining, traditional or innovative business activities. With the help of microfinance, debtors are able to become self-employed. They can thus lease a plot of land for cultivation, trade through a merchandise stall, or carry out artisanal work (such as weaving/dressmaking, making home/kitchen utensils, and so on), invest in means of production (for example, the acquisition of cattle or poultry; the purchase of seeds, fertilizers, or tools for producing and selling their merchandise.

Larger loans can be as much as US$20,000 per borrower to buy such equipment as a truck, a mechanical tiller, an irrigation pump, or a river craft; often, the loans are contracted by the wife and the equipment is operated by the husband. Grameen Bank and its emulators have helped their borrowers – mainly women – to escape confinement within their homes and empowered them to take part in the community's gainful activities. It has also enabled them to become more autonomous and better respected by their husbands as a result of their business initiatives, leading to a positive impact on marriage and family planning.

Microfinance vehicles – though not aiming at maximizing profits as sought by commercial financial institutions – have proved to be financially self-sufficient and economically viable in market economies by covering their costs. Their fundamental innovative feature is that they cater for deprived people who have no credit history, no predictable income, and no assets that could be subject to legal liens or used as collateral to guarantee their borrowing.

Creditworthiness of the poor is, in the absence of property, based on their high motivation and determination to become self-reliant and to succeed in their small business activities. They generally have an unwavering will to overcome – by their own honest efforts – their current conditions of misery, to repay their debts, and become economically autonomous and socially respected. This presumes that the microcredit borrowers are able to find remunerative market outlets for their products (see, for example, *The Economist*, 2005a). The microfinance model – using different variants – has been widely espoused in over 100 countries, both developing and developed, spanning multiple cultures.

The women majority of borrowers from the Grameen Bank (97 per cent) have had superior creditworthiness compared to men in the same socio-economic category. Prompted by self-development, women borrowers have demonstrated over time their capacity to manage their household resources thriftily, and to use the benefits of finance in upgrading the health–educational conditions of their families and the comfort and cleanliness of their homes. The financial empowerment of women has enabled them to overcome their traditionally downtrodden and subordinated status *vis-à-vis* men, to gain more control over their destiny, to contribute to their family's progress, and indirectly to the progress of society. One should caution that women borrowers could well act on behalf of their males in their families (husband, father or sons), who could use the extended credit on non-productive expenditure.

Grameen's organizational–operational approach informally assigns the function of screening, selection, monitoring, oversight and implementation of obligations – based on *suasion* – to teams of between five and twenty members of depositors or erstwhile borrowers from the local community. With no formal group guarantee or joint liability with binding instruments, the team's approach has proved optimal in cutting down on potential defaulters and urging rigour; it has yielded insightful peer review (for the selection of eligible borrowers) and peer pressure (for making the debtor keen to honour her/his obligations) to avoid being shamed. This approach of 'informal bonding' has favoured mutual understanding and the willingness to help other members in periods of difficulty. The exercise of peer discipline on borrowers has led to the productive use of funds and to financial discipline in the timely reimbursement of instalments – without the fear of bringing court proceedings against defaulters. Depositors and borrowers (who own 94 per cent of the Bank, with the remainder owned by the Bangladesh government) have thus been infused with the spirit of *informal solidarity*, to ensure the long-term economic viability of the Grameen Bank and its subsidiaries.

Terms of microfinance

Microfinance terms of lending are founded on a variety of principles (see Exhibit 1.1). The Grameen Bank does not subsidize loans apart from student loans and loans to beggars (called 'struggling members'), which bear 5 per cent and 0 per cent financial charges respectively. The bank's founder considers Grameen to be a social business, defined as 'a non-loss, non-dividend' project for investors, at the service of the poor (Muhammad Yunus, Nobel Prize lecture, 10 December 2006; http://nobelpeaceprize.org).

Exhibit 1.1 Microfinance's diversity of conditions (selected factors)

1 'Usurer' terms:
Exploit positions of monopoly power or political ascendancy.
2 'Commercial' terms:
Maximize profits while operating within competitive markets.
3 'Socially-responsible' terms:
A reasonable 'profit margin' is charged.
4 Sharing net return:
Net benefits accruing on the capital provided by the financier are split equally between the provider and the user of the capital.
5 Break-even terms:
These cover all costs, but exclude the profit margin.
6 Inclusive of a 'grant' factor:
These include a total or partial subsidy (with respect to interest or principal), generally for the benefit of disfavoured, destitute and/or disabled people.
7 Sources of funding:
(a) Private, governmental or mixed; and
(b) Domestic and/or foreign.
8 Selection of borrowers, disbursement and collection of funds:
(a) Watchdog function exercised by peers (depositors or erstwhile borrowers); and
(b) Disbursement and recovery of funds by instalment (to favour regular oversight over borrowers and/or to spread over time the financial charges).
9 Governmental regulation:
For licensing, setting principles and fixing rules (of prudential behaviour, transparency, reporting, competitive conduct, avoidance of abuse, among others).

Note: A 'full-cost' loan covers (i) cost of capital; (ii) operating costs of financial vehicles; (iii) credit risk; (iv) inflation risk; (v) market risk; (vi) exchange risk (for foreign-currency funds); (vii) sovereign/political/social risks; (viii) risks of eventual disasters, and other risks.

The Grameen Bank covers its costs by charging on average 20 per cent p.a. on its 'income generating loans', calculated on a 'declining basis' of the outstanding debt balance. The Grameen Bank and similar microfinance institutions have relatively high financial charges, since fixed administrative costs weigh heavily on small-size loans. Moreover, the Bank's collaborators visit the homes of borrowers to provide banking services, such as the disbursement of credit contracted and the collection – on a weekly basis – of reimbursements. The weekly collections are justified by the Bank's desire to instil in the behaviour of borrowers a measure of discipline in the use and repayment of loans. Microfinance institutions have generally been able to break even although charging considerably lower than usurers' rates that strangle the poor (see Yunus, 2009; also La Torre and Vento, 2006).

In the absence of microfinance institutions of the type described above, the poor are at the mercy of usurers who exploit their vulnerability. In incidents of bullying and humiliation of poor borrowers who could not meet their onerous financial obligations on time, individuals have in sheer desperation committed suicide – reportedly as many as 166,000 farmers in India over the period 1997–2007 (see, for example, 'India pledges £7.6bn to combat rural suicides', *guardian.co.uk*; and *The Economist*, 2006a). Millions of impoverished Indian farmers have been exploited by loan sharks forcing them into a 'financial serfdom' condition. This prompted the Indian government in 2008 to cancel the debt of some 30 million small farmers (each holding less than two hectares of land) contracted prior to 31 March 2007 – the scheme cost about US$17 billion (see *The Economist*, 2008a). Usurers' rates could well exceed 100 per cent per annum (i.e. several times estimated competitive commercial rates).

Microfinance institutions which charge 'commercial' (in lieu of the lower 'socially responsible') rates of interest can produce attractive returns for the benefit of their current investors and seek to entice potential investors. This was the case of the Mexican microfinance institution CompartamosBanco, whose yield on its gross loan portfolio was 79 per cent, and return on equity 46 per cent in 2007 (see CompartamosBanco, *A Letter to our peers*, by Carlos Danel & Carlos Labarthe, 17 June 2008, 14p.; also *The Economist*, 2008b). The bank was so lucrative that it went public (through an initial public offering – IPO) appealing to investors because of its high financial performance. Other promoters of microfinance vehicles have set up investment funds to appeal to a variety of institutional investors (see, for example, Dieckmann, 2007; www.finethic.org/fr/news and www.mixmarket.org). The potential of mobilizing capital at commercial rates is significant.

Generally, rates charged on microloans have ranged between 20 per cent and 35 per cent. They take into account debtor risk, as well as the erosion of money's purchasing power or inflation, country risk, and foreign exchange risk for internationally funded microcredit. Microfinance administrative fixed costs (for the identification, screening, processing, disbursement, monitoring, collection of repayment of loans and so on) are, compared to larger loans, relatively high in view of the small sums that are loaned to a widely scattered universe of poor borrowers in rural areas (see, for example, Kota, 2007; also Dellien *et al.*, 2005 available at: www.swwb.org).

From the standpoint of public interest, a measure of subsidization of interest is fully justified to the extent that significant *benefits of progress* spill over to the rest of society. These benefits come out in the form of: alleviation of poverty; empowerment of hitherto excluded segments of society; boosting of entrepreneurship; reduction of social tensions; improvements in health, education and housing. Some investors, such as pension funds, may not seek maximum returns from their investments in microfinance institutions. They will be content with a 'reasonable financial return', (see, for example, Mary Ellen Iskenderian, president and CEO of Women's World Banking, on www.microplaceblog.com; and BlueOrchard, Micro Investment Managers, on www.blueorchard.org).

Microfinance institutions do not have a one-size-fits-all model: their features vary with respect to terms of financing, organization, scope of activities, and other aspects. A key factor of differentiation is the cost of credit to potential borrowers. Capital providers can supply their resources at commercial or subsidized interest rates and can resort to different approaches or modalities to suit multiple socio-economic conditions (see, for example, Vogel and Hayes, 1998). At one end of the spectrum are low-income people willing and able to pay reasonable commercial charges obtaining in the market place, while at the other end of the spectrum are the destitute (for reasons of health, natural disasters, exclusion, or others) or the financially bonded. The latter need to be subsidized or freed from financial bondage for charitable/humane reasons (see, for example, van Doorn and Churchill, 2004).

Overall, the leading developer of the now globally known microfinance phenomenon – Muhammad Yunus – has won wide acclaim, including the 2006 Nobel Prize for Peace, shared by him and the Grameen Bank he established. Microfinance has thus provided the very poor with vital financial services – notably loans at reasonable terms, and deposit and transaction facilities – rendering this phenomenon an economically viable proposition. The rate of loan recovery has been an astounding 99 per cent (see the Nobel Lecture given by Muhammad Yunus in Oslo, 10 December 2006; available at: http://nobelpeaceprize.org).

Microfinance has opened new vistas to borrowers – helping them to overcome their destitution through the productive employment of borrowed money, thereby reducing sources of potential violence and conflict within communities, and promoting social harmony in many countries. As stated by the Norwegian Nobel Committee, Muhammad Yunus and the Grameen Bank have contributed to lasting peace by enabling 'large population groups to find ways to break out of poverty ... Development from below also serves to advance democracy and human rights.'

An innovative successful enterprise generally becomes a source of emulation. This has happened to the Grameen Bank, which has seen the growth of other microcredit institutions in Bangladesh (such as BRAC and ASA) and beyond in both developed and developing economies. Among subsequent microfinance innovations, one could mention Kiva (meaning 'agreement' in Swahili), an organization that enables individual creditors – anywhere in the world – to lend directly (person to person) and readily (via a computer system) to a poor entrepreneur among a large number of candidates vetted with the help of a local microfinance partner institution. The lender uses his/her credit card via the internet, for the fund's disbursement and collection, and can follow in regular transparent reporting the deployment of the loan, whose term usually extends up to 8–12 months (see www.kiva.org). While the lender does not receive interest on the loan, the borrower pays a charge to defray some of Kiva's costs.

Entrepreneurial 'complementary' activities

The strategy of opening up the productive potential of the poor can be shored up by multiple services provided to this hitherto neglected or exploited category of humanity. It is normal to start with complementary services to credit (deposit taking, transfers, insurance, investment and others). Beyond these services, it is worthwhile noting that Yunus and his team at the Grameen Bank have expanded into other areas, in association with international groups – notably food products (with Danon), information technologies and telecommunications (with Telenor), potable water (with Veolia), energy, textiles and other domains of interest to his customer base. Such an expansion has the advantage of offering the poor, on reasonable terms, other much-needed goods or services and of diversifying the risks of the bank.

As the Grameen Bank's founder has become increasingly absorbed on international travel and other long absences, and as his initial collaborators have aged, rejuvenation to maintain dynamism and promote innovativeness attuned to changing social/technological environments has become imperative to sustain further expansion. Some observers consider that he promoted a 'certain cult of his personality', though one could say more appropriately that he promoted his projects for the benefit of his constituency (see, for example, Ram Etwareea, 2008).

As a logical complement to his mission of overcoming poverty, he decided in February 2007 to set up a political party for socio-economic reforms founded on an all-inclusive democracy, ethical values and justice. His goal of societal progress has thus prompted him to seek to complete his work at the microfinance level by attempting to reform his country's institutions – ensuring the proper functioning of a sound and corruption-free political system in the best interest of all citizens. His political ambitions have nevertheless floundered on encountering a lack of interest among targeted participants. One could well refer also to the scepticism of rivals, and the powerful resistance of dominant clans, embedded politicians with narrow partisan interests, or the opposition of the military establishment in his strife-torn country.

'Financial discipline' and 'material collaterals'

Historical evidence shows that lending to the poor who exercise prudence and financial discipline – as presented above – carries a lesser risk or *superior safety* for lenders, compared to borrowers offering physical collateral but lacking financial discipline. This can be illustrated by reference to the 2007–9 debacle in the US housing market (see, for example, Andrew Felton and Carmen M. Reinhart (eds), 2008; available at: www.voxeu.org). Financial intermediaries were ready and willing then to lend borrowers with low creditworthiness (subprime). Prior to the debacle, euphoric borrowers and lenders expected (unrealistically) a continuous rise in house prices to allow borrowers to refinance their due financial charges with additional borrowing (see Ellis, 2008).

Collateralized borrowers can fail if they contract loans in excess of the realistic value of their properties and/or in excess of their income capacity-cum-willingness to service their debt charges (payment of interest and reimbursement of principal). The subprime situation also reflects laxity on the part of lenders who eased their lending standards and documentation requirements excessively. Physical collaterals can, indeed, sour and lose in market value. Loan originators were hardly concerned with credit risk, since they severed their links to borrowers by not holding the mortgage loans to maturity. Originators of subprime mortgage loans were interested in generating fees and commissions: they packaged, structured, securitized and sold collateralized debt obligations (CDOs) backed by portfolios of mortgage loans. Investors were pension funds, insurance companies, off-balance-sheet special-purpose vehicles (SPVs) of banks, and others, in the USA and beyond. Banks' SPVs are not subject to regulator's supervision or capital adequacy requirements (see, for example, Norges Bank, 2007).

Lenders or investors in the US housing sector in the early 21st century had thus generally failed to exercise discipline and prudence in assessing, pricing and monitoring risks, and in controlling misleading acts or practices. The measures or models of risk of the financial intermediaries involved in the US subprime products have proved to be flawed (notably with respect to creditworthiness and liquidity risk). Several lenders/investors/guarantors/underwriters, furthermore, had excessive exposure to, and poor knowledge of, subprime products compared to other banking activities. This explains the multibillion-dollar credit-related losses they sustained, notably over the period 2007–9 after the collapse of the US housing market (see, for example, Yellen, 2008; Dodd, 2007; Fender and Hördahl, 2007; also *The Economist*, 2007b).

It is disturbing to realize that the world's leading financial intermediaries had over 2007–9 within their asset portfolios relatively excessive concentrations of risky instruments (mainly related to the subprime mortgage products). Such a situation blatantly contradicts their own declared 'sound risk-management principles'. Indeed, they failed in properly screening their loans or investments, in pricing their risks, and in diversifying their assets judiciously. By comparison, the management and customers of microfinance institutions of certain developing countries – notably the Grameen Bank mentioned above – have behaved responsibly and rigorously in controlling risks, despite the fact that their borrowers are much poorer than borrowers in the USA. Moreover, the managers of reputed microfinance institutions have not allowed personal greed or deceit to affect their behaviour or taint their judgement.

Case C: Migration and community revitalization

The entrepreneurial case analysed below represents an original model to counter dangerous and illegal emigration from a poor country in favour of gainful work in one's homeland. The entrepreneur in question abandoned material satisfaction and comfort in a developed society to create some material/spiritual satisfaction in his desolate community of origin. His efforts have paid off thanks to his work ethos, as has been shown afterwards.

Challenges

Migratory flows have been common throughout history. The appeal of prosperous countries to outsiders is evident. Many people (mainly young adults) despairing of finding work or a safe life in their homelands, have sought to leave their troubled countries. Their reasons have been varied, economic or non-economic – such as endemic unemployment, wars and violence, tyranny, persecution, discrimination and injustice, famine, ecological disasters, moral misery, and others. Lured by the dream of a better life in an advanced, stable country, illegal migration has proved to be dangerous, and subject to many obstacles – including those set by retrenched 'citadels of prosperity' bent on blocking or containing the influx of aliens.

Illegal migrants have been turned back at borders, detained, imprisoned, deported or allowed to die (often drowning in treacherous seas, or perishing in harsh lands). Several thousand fatalities among migrants have occurred in recent years, and the tragic conditions of loss of life have occasionally aroused criticism by the public when they have been reported by various media. The humiliation, extortion or other mistreatment endured by illegal migrants have been widespread. Cruelty has been encountered in their countries of origin, the countries they pass through, and eventually wherever they have been able to land – if they survive.

Asylum seekers and illegal migrants often face brutalization by security forces and abuses by criminal traffickers in this 'trade in human beings'. These traffickers mislead credulous people with false hopes, rob them of their belongings, including their savings, and abandon them before they reach the border – as has reliably been reported in well-documented research papers, articles or books (see, for example, Refugee Studies Centre, 2006–7, available at www.rsc.ox.ac.uk; also Gatti, 2008). Traffickers smuggle wretched migrants on ill-equipped journeys over treacherous routes (seas, deserts, mountains, swamps and forests, evading interdictions or tackling physical barriers such as electrified barbed wire, high sand or cement walls, military fortifications and so on). Crammed into rickety boats or unsafe vehicles, many would-be migrants have perished in hostile environments before reaching their destination.

Surviving illegal migrants reaching their countries of destination or passage are confronted to the trauma of being (a) stigmatized, tracked down, rounded-up, detained and humiliated as a result of their ethnic-cultural or racial backgrounds, and eventually deported to their country of origin (which is often a failed state); (b) forced to live in fear clandestinely in the country they reach; or (c) driven into criminal activities. If they find work, it is often as fugitives in the underground economy or in precarious odd jobs carried out in bleak, unsafe conditions with no holidays or social cover. In the latter case, unscrupulous employers choose to exploit illegal immigrants' vulnerability through miserly pay, hard labour, insalubrious crowded housing, dangerous or harsh working conditions, while denying them medical protection and proper education for their children.

Illegal migrants' fleeting, mirage-like expectations of prosperity in safe countries have often turned out to be pipe dreams. One official – Oumar Hamadoun Dicko (Minister for Malians Residing Abroad and African Integration) had pleaded for an alleviation of the desperate conditions encountered by African migrants. He also referred to 'the economic and sexual exploitation of migrant women and children; in the unfair trade practices that wrecked development in poor countries;

in the divisive and deceptive media and their portrayal of the West as an "El Dorado-like" paradise; in the shameless exploitation of clandestine immigrants working in poor and hazardous conditions for little money; and especially in the huge commissions charged by institutions sending and receiving remittances' (see Dicko, 2006).

Migrants' misfortunes can also be attributed to their countries' despotic self-serving rulers who have eviscerated national economies and undermined their growth potential (for example, by burdening them with excessive debt and/or stifling them with corruption). These rulers have also failed in introducing appropriate socio-economic institutions that allow for fair treatment of all members of society to unlock their creative potentialities. Furthermore, iniquitous and cruel mores/traditions or arbitrary practices have disenfranchised or enslaved important segments of society – thus depriving them of their identity and forcing them into the status of outcasts with no opportunity for justice or progress. Efficient and fair administrations, along with judicious socio-economic policies, are necessary prerequisites for progress.

Combining business and spiritual leadership

Bearing in mind the difficult context discussed above, it is interesting to consider the entrepreneurial venture of the Senegalese national, Serigne Babacar Mbow, who has been spurred by his deeply-felt need to lift his people from destitution via business creativity, responsibility and hard work. His ultimate objective is to enable each person in his community to attain a dignified life of satisfaction. His original type of entrepreneurship has been underpinned by the spiritual teachings and values of his forebears. These are edifying African luminaries who belong to the Mouridiya brotherhood, a mystical branch of Islam. Their piety is based on the precepts of charity, tolerance, non-violence and, most importantly, *toil*. Humility, unremitting work, self-reliance and solidarity on Earth pave the way to paradise – according to that brotherhood's teachings (see, for example, Audrain, 2002; also *The Economist*, 2006b; Labarthe, 2008).

Mbow's drive, combining spiritual values with entrepreneurship, has placed zeal for 'creative relentless work, discipline, and moral conscientiousness' in a superior central position, akin to other orthodox tenets of piety, such as praying and fasting. His work ethos thus makes 'productive/profit-making toil' a source of salvation of the highest spiritual value, in so far as such a way of life lifts humankind from a state of destitution, servility and misery into one of decent living and dignity. Instead of witnessing passively the debilitating exodus of human resources from the region of his forebears and allowing his community to languish in desolation, trapped by misery, Mbow and his companions have braced themselves to open up business opportunities for their people in their native land, and to rejuvenate their community. They have encouraged young migrants to return to the fold, to live in freedom from want and/or abuse, and lead a dignified, productive life away from the dangers of inhospitable alien lands.

Guided by his humane values, Mbow, joined by his wife of French extraction, resolved in 1984 to leave the material comfort of France where he had emigrated in search of education and professional success and return to Senegal to live in his native village, Ndem, despite the fact that it had almost been abandoned by its people after decades of drought and neglect. Believing in the prospects of his homeland, Mbow's goal is to create a thriving '*space for business opportunities*' in his birthplace, with ripple effects beyond – generating new business activities that will sustain progress to the benefit of all participants.

When making vital decisions, Mbow has relied on the dedication of his Parisian wife and partner, Pascale Blanchard. The latter, on choosing to join the Mouridiya community, adopted the name of Aïssa (a typical local name). Her separation from the material comfort of Paris, where she was born and reared, has not prevented her from enjoying a happy, meaningful life in Ndem – despite its frugality – because of the spiritual teachings of the new faith she has espoused and the welcoming solidarity of her adoptive community (see Dia (a cultural journalist in Dakar-Senegal) 2000; available at: http://www.pimkey.com/-toilemet/tmag6/habiller6.htm).

Mbow's wife contributed to helping him realize his vision by giving all her material resources to their new venture. Sharing an austere African hut with their children in an almost deserted village has reportedly not dismayed the couple, nor denied them an inner sense of happiness. Indeed, Ndem and other villages in the immediate vicinity (fourteen in total) did not on their arrival have any basic facilities, such as schools or healthcare (see Delorme, 2005; also www.ong-ndem.org).

With the strong support of trusted followers, Mbow and his wife prepared themselves for a tough challenge to realize their shared vision. With his wife's sewing machine (the only equipment they had to start with), Mbow launched a workshop making traditional garments (*niaxass* – a tunic of multicoloured patchwork) with the help of two tailors he had invited to return home from the capital city, Dakar, to their native village. Moreover, he has been the linchpin in forming a network of several partners, the co-operative 'Association of the Villagers of Ndem' (AVN) to organize and develop a thriving business hub and build the necessary infrastructure (with some external contributions). AVN's ultimate objective is to create a business hub for artisans with a special 'cachet of excellence' (see Roy, 1998; available at: http://membres.lycos.fr/ndem/presse.htm). AVN's fourteen villages (totalling over 3,000 inhabitants), including Ndem, embraced some 300 artisans in 2006. Members' monthly contributions have averaged half a dollar. In addition, Aïssa's parents – notably her mother Geneviève Marotte – opened a boutique in the Marais district of Paris to serve as a major outlet in France for the sale of Mbow's products.

Mbow's venture (called 'Maam Samba' after the name of his grandfather) has succeeded in attracting several Senegalese expatriates to return from Europe. Mathioro Ndiya is one of them. With a master's degree from the Sorbonne in Paris and after nine years working in France, he decided to return to his native land to join Mbow's local craft firm (employing more than 360 people) as a public relations (PR) representative. Such voluntary repatriation illustrates eloquently the phenomenon of reversing the 'human-power drain', from a developed country to the developing home country of origin. At a time when his community was faced with a dwindling population resulting from an exodus of people to the capital city of Dakar and overseas, in a quest for a decent livelihood, Maam Samba is a tribute to its entrepreneurial founder (www.maam-samba.com). Mbow has spread among members of his community the ethos of assuming a productive existence through developing and promoting (a) local artisans' special *know-how*; and (b) local artists' ingenious designs. This combination has created a competitive edge for the community's original and high-quality goods – which are regenerated continuously.

Mbow's business leadership – as an initiator of a business project, and as an assembler and motivator of collaborators – has enabled him to stimulate villagers into forming a closely-knit cluster or hub of artisans and artists. They produce high-quality hand-made cotton clothes and household items in Ndem, within the region of Diourbel located some 120 km (about 75 miles) from Senegal's capital city, Dakar. His hub-like business model has attracted complementary activities, and allowed consumer products to move up the value chain. Mbow's business model has been emulated by some thirty-four other neighbouring villages. The end products of the hub cover several domains, notably textiles (cloth-making, laces and other accessories), household utensils, furniture, paintings and drawings, decorative items, dolls and statuettes, metal and pottery work, musical instruments, leather goods (bags, wallets, shoes and so on), carpets and other items. The Maam Samba artisans (some 60 per cent of them women) produce stylish or fashionable custom-made products, as well as ready-made ones catering for both national and foreign markets (mainly chic boutiques in Europe and North America). One of the first sales outlets – so vital to Mbow's mission – was his mother-in-law, who until her retirement marketed his products successfully in France.

It is interesting to note that AVN's sales outlets (in Senegal, Europe and North America) have welcomed customer suggestions for widening the spectrum of products. Thanks to a rapid reactivity to customers' wishes, Mbow and the AVN members have adopted a novel strategy of developing creativity, based on *cross-fertilizing* three factors: (a) the talent of native artists and designers; combined with (b) high-quality craftsmanship using innovative local resources (such as indigenous textile dyeing); and underpinned by (c) toil, steadfastness, tenacity and conscientiousness. Original products have thus been produced that appeal to consumers in Europe and North America for their artistic/traditional quality value. The brand name of Ndem as a source of high-quality artistic crafts has thus been built up, giving its artisans an advantage *vis-à-vis* competitors in Africa and beyond (for factors of competitive advantage, see Exhibit 1.2).

Mbow and his associates and collaborators in AVN have thus adopted a strategy of *vertical integration*, linking market outlets (boutiques as well as pedlars from the Mouridiya brotherhood) to production units. This strategy allows for a rapid transmission of customers' requirements to production units, and ensures the optimal satisfaction of customers' wishes. Such links are vital for acting speedily on the wishes of current and potential buyers with respect to variety, styles and quality of products required. Such requests collected *downstream* at sales points could then be followed up (by designers and

Exhibit 1.2 Selected factors of a firm's competitiveness

1 Compared to its competitors, the firm's products face a relatively inelastic demand (for such reasons as their: superior quality, utility or efficiency, which cannot easily be replicated; reliable after-sales services; ready response to customers' changing needs).
2 Management's judicious strategies make use of its talented, entrepreneurial and motivated personnel to sustain its competitive edge (through training and innovation; diversification; integration of promising entities; spin-off (i.e. divest) unattractive activities; rigorous effective controls of risks, costs and quality; and other relevant means).
3 The firm has easy access to funding and other inputs at reasonable terms – with suppliers and contractors not in a position to exploit monopolistic situations.
4 The firm enjoys superior production/distribution/marketing advantages compared to competitors, and its sales do not encounter dominant buyers who exploit their superior bargaining power.
5 The firm applies corporate governance, and complies with regulatory prescriptions (health/sanitary, labour/social, fiscal, environmental, and others).

Notes:
1. Hypotheses: the listed factors exclude predatory/cut-throat competition, and governmental regulations and policies affecting business activities apply without discrimination.
2. Studies on competitiveness are legion. Sources include empirical research by academic centres, as well as professional institutes affiliated to business organizations (covering time series for economic sectors in several countries). Among notable academic references, one can mention Porter, 1998; and Porter and Kramer, 2006.

craft-workers) at production points *upstream.* Mbow's strategies of *vertical integration,* coupled with *product diversification* aimed at tapping into a wide spectrum of consumers' markets have demonstrated their productivity. This has led to enhancing the reputation of AVN for a variety of products, catering for the different needs of a widening circle of customers.

As a result of their profit-making activities, stakeholders (artisans and the various other parties in AVN) have allocated a significant portion of their resources and/or time to the construction and running of schools, maternity and health care centres, a microcredit vehicle and other essential infrastructures. External contributors have helped the local community in: repairing or drilling wells to tap ground-water aquifers to meet the population's needs for drinking water; transforming some of the hitherto barren lands affected by drought and poor soil into cultivable arable land as a result of drip-irrigated gardens; installing solar energy devices for the generation of cheap local power; arranging for means of transport; building and running elementary schools and community clinics; and others (see also 'Docey Lewis and Senegalese Textile Artisans, June 2007' – available at www.aidtoartisans.org).

Craft shops have sprung up to weave local cotton from the region, dyeing textiles with the traditional African *bogolan* technique using indigenous materials (local mud, clay and ash mixed with herbs and leaves from surrounding bush lands, as a cheap and ecologically-respectful alternative to chemical dyes). This method of dyeing has attracted an increasingly large circle of customers sensitive to the priority of protecting the environment. Other techniques of dyeing are also used, such as batik. Nevertheless, despite the marketing campaigns by Senegalese entrepreneurs, the large market potential of AVN's artistic/artisanal works has yet to be fully exploited, notwithstanding the international appeal of authentic and original high-quality African articles (see Skelton, 2006; *Senegal sect's work ethic brings stability, prosperity,* 2006 at www.seneweb.com; Jallow, 1996, available at www.djembe.dk/no/16seneg1.html; and Association des Villageois de Ndem, available at: www.ong-ndem.org).

To conclude, Mbow and his artisans have created value based on five main pillars of competitiveness:

(i) household articles which appeal to a diverse range of customers;
(ii) fashionable designs combining artistic beauty with tradition;
(iii) use of non-toxic local inputs which respect human health and ecology;
(iv) efficient and customer-responsive small-scale production; and

(v) direct peddling or marketing – nationally and internationally – by members of the community and/or motivated sympathizers.

Interpreting the quintessence of entrepreneurship

Entrepreneurs such as those profiled briefly above are particularly driven by two basic considerations: (i) benefits to various stakeholders within their business entities; and (ii) the promotion of ethical values and societal progress. The entrepreneurs cited share a vision of life that goes beyond the sole motivation of 'pecuniary personal gain'; they have all aspired to transform their respective society's way of living for the better. Entrepreneurs in advanced market economies have generally enjoyed an encouraging regulatory environment for their development. However, this is not the case for entrepreneurs in poor economics – such as Bangladesh and Senegal – who have had to battle against great odds and harsh environments.

Two of the three examples of entrepreneurs mentioned above were founded and nurtured by the active involvement of *married couples:* Mbow and Ovshinky. These are examples of family-owned businesses or projects (FBs). This is notably the case with Serigne Babacar Mbow's business, created in Senegal with the support of his wife Aïssa; this Afro-European couple, along with their six children, favoured the challenge of their entrepreneurial mission in Senegal over the comfort of their previous home in Paris. All entrepreneurs studied believe in, and work for, the empowerment of women in business as a means of progress. For example Stan and Iris Ovshinsky set up the ECD venture in 1960 and worked together for some fifty years until Iris's death in 2006, also raising five children. An interviewer quoted Iris: 'As Stan said, the shared values are so important. We founded ECD with the express purpose of using science and technology to solve serious societal problems' to which Stan added: 'We just work together in everything. And there's just Stan-Iris, or Iris-Stan' (see Villiger, 2004).

Several research centres (academic or linked to business groups) and international or regional organizations (such as the World Bank, the OECD or the European Union) have been interested in identifying the quintessence of entrepreneurship. An academically-sponsored research consortium (covering national teams from more than forty countries) offers a broad definition in their Global Entrepreneurship Monitor (GEM). Their research data and analyses refer to 'entrepreneurship' as a process covering the role played by individuals at different phases, extending

> from the very early phase when businesses are in gestation to the established phase and possibly discontinuation of the business ... Someone who is just starting a venture and trying to make it in a very competitive market is an entrepreneur in spite of not having high-growth aspirations. On the other hand, a person may be an established business owner who has been in business for quite a number of years and still be innovative, competitive, and growth minded. This person is also an entrepreneur.

This definition is centred on individuals who may have a wide variety of entrepreneurial characteristics, motivations or approaches to creating value (see Bosma *et al.*, 2008; also www.gemconsortium.org).

Creative entrepreneurs, like those described above, are diverse. Yet they share the urge to change the status quo by exploiting perceived business opportunities or providing workable solutions to problems or difficulties. Their success is realized though (a) the launching of new, higher-quality products; or (b) adopting efficient business strategies, methods or instruments. They apply their know-how to produce new goods or services that appeal to consumers or users, and generate benefits for the parties concerned. Superior innovations are recognized by a combination of criteria: novelty; significant and enduring value creation; positive externalities; and the potential to unlock additional innovations. To develop their innovations, entrepreneurs critically need appropriate funding, as empirical studies have demonstrated (see, for example, Meyer, 2008).

While some entrepreneurs can also be inventors – that is, creators of new goods or services (which can be subject to patenting), other entrepreneurs develop and commercialize the ideas and products conceived by others. Inventors can (a) operate independently and sell their 'intellectual property rights' to entrepreneurs; or (b) be recruited by entrepreneurs with an employment contract providing attractive incentives – both financial and non-financial. Entrepreneurial businesses based on technology are generally recognized by a relatively high percentage of the firm's total expenditure being devoted to research and development (R&D) – leading eventually to *patented* products. Holders of patents (whether acquired or internally developed within firms) enjoy legal exclusive commercialization rights, nationally or internationally, over relatively long periods (for example, twenty years). Patents are protected, and those responsible for pirating, counterfeiting or plundering them are prosecuted and sanctioned. The edge of a technical innovator over competitors can be measured by the length of time (years or months) his competitors need before they can emulate or surpass his/her products.

Those who start businesses may have diverse motives. Often, entrepreneurs are prompted by either (a) the enticement of sizeable profits generated by the drive to exploit a perceived promising business opportunity; or (b) the imperative necessity to be independently self-employed, often after losing a regular job. The former motive – the exploitation of a business opportunity – reflects the creative drive of genuine entrepreneurs, while the latter motive – employment – reflects a need to compensate for the loss of a regular job and salary. Indeed, the mere search for an activity to compensate for traditional employment does not generally end up in innovative start-ups with promising growth potential, and is likely to take the form of a conventional activity, such as running a shop or a food outlet (see, for example, Meyer, 2007).

Entrepreneurial drive can lead to the revitalization of previously neglected or languishing communities, via the introduction of new, 'economically viable' business activities. This can be illustrated by an entrepreneur who uses appropriate techniques to reclaim barren land to make it cultivable and capable of launching an agro-business. *Economic value* is not premised solely on technological breakthroughs with novel products or means of production: it can also be generated from a better-performing 'organization and operation' of the enterprise through the redeployment of existing resources and skills. Entrepreneurs can thus enhance the quality or efficiency of their products or processes, and their efficient delivery to users and consumers – resulting from cumulative improvements in one or more business functions such as marketing, production, finance, transport, and distribution, among others (see, for example, Kanter, 2006).

Traits of entrepreneurship are complex, vary in importance or style from one entrepreneur to another, and are influenced by their sociocultural environment. Nevertheless, the basic traits mentioned above are more common among the younger adult generation (25 to 34 years of age) who are likely to be looking more positively to the future (*GEM*). These individuals are thus more inclined to take risks in creating their early-stage enterprises – whether personally-owned, family-owned or partnered with similar people. Nevertheless, individuals at relatively advanced ages can still have a 'creative' mind and prove their entrepreneurial fibre.

Far from being lumped into stereotypes or clichés, each entrepreneur has genuine personal qualities and idiosyncrasies. Indeed, an authentic leader – whether in business or in other realms of human endeavour – has a unique personality, often influenced by a myriad of factors linked to the inner self and the socio-geographical environment (see, for example, George *et al.*, 2007; Badaracco, 2006; *The Economist*, 2009). Nevertheless, distilling from the above case studies the shared basic traits of successful progress-driven entrepreneurs, four intertwined characteristics appear clearly to be significant. These are:

1 *A vision of novelty combined with pragmatism.* Entrepreneurs are individuals recognized by a clear *vision* for realizing business opportunities. Their creativity is coupled with a practical skill for implementation, usually underpinned by sound long-term planning and strategy. Because of their pragmatism, they are capable of pursuing their ideas (for example, starting with prototypes for technological innovations) until they reach operational profitability. Entrepreneurs are *catalysts of change*, innovating in their chosen field by challenging conventional ways of thinking and working. They are characterized by an independent and resourceful spirit, though they are often considered sceptically by their community as *maverick* or *unorthodox* people bent on changing the status quo.
2 *Motivation and a proclivity for risk.* Entrepreneurs are generally prompted by a compelling dedication to realize their projects – for themselves, as well as for the benefit of stakeholders. With *passion, zest* and *determination*, they are carried along by their own impetus regardless of constraints and the hostility of vested interests or envious rivals. Entrepreneurs are, indeed, *daring* people who operate in uncertain, dynamic environments. Their *audacity* enables them to seize business opportunities through untried paths. This involves *bravery* in crossing the Rubicon by taking substantial risks – through committing all their personal resources

(capital, technical–organizational talent, relentless hard work, and reputation) to their projects – thus overcoming fear of failure. Their *risk appetite* is considerable (or, put differently, their *risk aversion* is low) in view of their passion for their project.

3 *Staying power and resilience.* Thanks to their *unwavering* purpose, they address challenges positively and overcome obstacles, prompted by an unabated enthusiasm for their vocation. As a result of their *grit*, successful entrepreneurs are not easily deflected by unexpected impediments; their stamina and resolve enable them to endure tremendous work pressure and stress with exceptional fortitude. Thanks to their self-discipline and their steadfastness, resilient entrepreneurs are capable of solving problems and rebounding with *agility* and *flexibility* from setbacks. Entrepreneurs do not grow *ex nihilo.* Whether self-taught or formally educated, entrepreneurs therefore need to have a large capacity for continuous *learning* and *improving* in a changing world – with patience and perseverance. The self-development process is founded on learning from past and current achievements as well as from failures.

4 *Significance of achievements.* A progress-driven entrepreneur's accomplishments are measured by reference to 'lasting and significant net benefits' for him/ herself as well as for other stakeholders – notably investors, creditors, collaborators/employees, customers, partners and the community. Negative externalities of a business activity (such as pollution, the degradation of health or quality of life, waste or harmful products) reduce the net benefits. Exemplary entrepreneurs are therefore recognized by *seminal* activities that open up potential new opportunities for other entrepreneurs to emulate, and for society to benefit from their contributions.

Entrepreneurs usually benefit from the emotional–psychic support of family (notably their spouse) and/or friends. Several academics or mentors of business leaders think that innovation and entrepreneurial talents can be developed (see, for example, Drucker, 1985; and Christensen and Raynor, 2003). For a groomer of business talents, 'natural entrepreneurs' are not the norm: leading an 'enterprise is a skill in itself, and it can be taught, and learnt' (see Russell Smith, cited in Lunnon, 2007). Expressed differently, 'an individual does not have to be born with any universal characteristics or traits of a leader ... Authentic leaders work hard at understanding and developing themselves' (see George *et al.*, 2007). Generally leadership/entrepreneurial talents are latent in human beings and can be drawn out, stimulated and developed with the help of mentors, technical advisors and strategic workshops (see Linda Rottenberg, founder of Endeavor Global at: www.endeavor.org).

Some business achievers – such as the television star and serial entrepreneur Peter Jones, supported by politicians (British prime minister Gordon Brown and his government) – believe that 16 to 19-year-olds can be taught how to be entrepreneurial. Jones and Brown have agreed jointly to launch and fund the National Enterprise Academy, to teach teenagers entrepreneurial skills in a 9-month programme combining academic disciplines and workshops (starting with a select number of 200 students). Jones intends to have a venture capital fund attached to the academy that will invest in the students' ideas (see Tyler, 2008). Nevertheless, entrepreneurial teaching will not come to fruition by simple inculcation – the people being taught must have a kernel of enterprising spirit waiting to be unlocked.

The highly desirable traits of entrepreneurship mentioned above are seldom all found, or found in equal importance, within a single person. Moreover, the ultimate success of an entrepreneurial project cannot be attributed solely to the entrepreneur. It is bound to be linked to multiple factors – chief among these being the enthusiastic support of colleagues and collaborators in a stimulating work environment. These collaborators can be strongly motivated by incentives of participation in the capital and/or profits of the firm to reward their performance. Entrepreneurs can, furthermore, test their newly developed products advantageously on their current (and potential) customers (see, for example, IBM, 2006a).

Size of business, entrepreneurship and growth

Definitions

International comparisons of correlations between *business size* on one hand, and *entrepreneurship, growth* or *job creation* on the other hand, need to be qualified for multiple important reasons such as differences in: definitions and measures of size; legal organization of firms; regulatory requirements; governmental incentives (fiscal, financial, or otherwise); and market conditions, e.g. unhampered access to financing (and other inputs) or sales outlets (see, for example, Katharina Hohmann, 'Dynamic diversity opens up opportunities – an international assessment of SMEs', Deutsche Bank Research, 15 April 2009, 23pp.).

For the European Commission, the size of an enterprise can be defined by its number of employees: micro (0–9), small (10–49), medium (50–249), and large (250+). Micro, small and medium-sized enterprises (referred to hereafter as SMEs) are also defined as those that have an annual turnover not exceeding 2, 10 and 50 million euros, respectively; and an annual balance sheet total not exceeding 2, 10 and 43 million euros, respectively (European Commission, 2003). SMEs in the European Union accounted for around 99 per cent of business units in 2006, providing some 75 million jobs (see *Eurostat:* http://ec.europa.eu/eurostat).

European SME units are further identified in relation to ownership. Four major categories of companies are defined. They comprise:

(i) completely *independent* ownership;
(ii) *autonomous* (whose capital is not held by more than 25 per cent by another company, and conversely that the company itself does not hold more than 25 per cent of another company's capital);
(iii) *partner* companies (if the percentages held in another company exceed 25 per cent but are below 50 per cent); and
(iv) *linked* companies if the ownership exceeds the above-mentioned ceiling.

The utility of these distinctions for the European Commission is to ascertain the need and eligibility for state-sponsored support, in the absence of other sources of finance. Compared to an independent or an autonomous company, it is realistic to assume that a *partner* company has more ready access to capital and other resources – often at favourable terms – from their related companies. This access becomes automatic for a *linked* company, which is an integral part of the *group* that controls it (directly or indirectly).

In the United Kingdom, small businesses represent more than two-thirds of total businesses. As a group, SMEs generally represent, in market economies, a substantial portion of national employment, gross domestic product (GDP), and exports. A considerable portion of SMEs belong to the FB (family business) category or have significant ownership stakes that belong to descendants of the founding entrepreneurs (see *The Economist*, 2004). In the USA, there are over 20 million SMEs, representing more than 90 per cent of US business enterprises in 2004. Definitions of size in the USA refer to employees: 'small' covers up to 500 employees for most manufacturing and mining industries, and 100 for all wholesale trade industries. With respect to sales, SMEs must not exceed US$31 million for construction industries, US$13 million for services and US$6.5 million for agriculture (see various publications of the US *Small Business Administration*; available at: *www.sba.gov/financing/size*).

It has been estimated that the average lifespan for a first-generation FB (founded, owned and managed by individuals or couples) is less than twenty-five years. For a variety of reasons (notably a lack of vocation or professionalism), less than 33 per cent of the FBs make it to the second generation through siblings; about 15 per cent make it to the third generation through cousins; and only 3 per cent of the extended family beyond that (see, for example, Naffziger *et al.*, 1999; and Linnermann, 2007d). The need to find an optimal succession path is thus paramount to assure the smooth transfer of ownership and management, and the further development of business operations. Some family business owners may sacrifice the growth of their businesses in order to retain ownership and management within the family circle. Alternatively, others accept a dilution of ownership and the loss of managerial control to industrial or financial groups, to accelerate business growth and value creation (see, for example, the case study in Yee, 2008). Private equity (PE) funds can be an attractive vehicle for an efficient transfer of ownership. PE investments cover early-stage (incubation and start-up) businesses, SMEs (micro, small and medium-sized), sizeable established businesses, and restructured enterprises (see chapter 2).

Potential of small entrepreneurial businesses

Typically, and compared to sizeable enterprises, small enterprises – notably start-ups – have 'shallow pockets' of financial resources. Capital (even relatively small amounts as that available through microfinance) can fuel the entrepreneurial spirit of SME owner-managers. The contribution of such entrepreneurs to creativity and to national wealth is, indeed, relatively more significant in a society whose social-educational values and institutional frameworks favour the emergence of small/medium-sized enterprises (SMEs). For example, small businesses in the USA – according to the US Small Business Administration – have produced over ten times more US-registered patents per employee than have large firms (see IBM, 2006b).

Innovation is likely to be higher in markets where numerous entrepreneurial small or medium-sized enterprises are active, compared to a situation of concentrated markets controlled by a few oligopolistic enterprises. It is generally recognized that limited access to capital and credit at reasonable terms is one of the key obstacles to the survival of small enterprises. Without adequate assets or guarantees to offer to traditional bankers, capital could be provided by informal parties – such as family, friends or business 'angels'. The latter are wealthy individuals and erstwhile business leaders who provide capital in return for a significant share in the equity of promising seed or start-up enterprises. They often accompany (with advice and business contacts) investee companies, coaching and passing on their expertise and experience to the entrepreneurs concerned. Other providers of capital are institutional parties – such as PE firms, which are examined in Part 2 of this book. All capital providers are enticed by potentially higher levels of expected returns on their investments, commensurate with the risks assumed.

Risks encountered by SMEs explain the much higher bankruptcy probabilities they face compared to larger firms, whether in periods of economic expansion or contraction (Norges Bank, 2005). Among these risks, one could mention the notable fact that the survival of these enterprises often depends on one person's situation (health, drive, innovativeness, managerial capacity and so on). Other handicaps relate to their limited access to other resources, both material (notably capital) and human (notably talents and skills). Indeed, access to capital on reasonable terms is crucial to the performance of an enterprise in so far as (a) finance is fungible – capable of being readily exchangeable into other resources; and (b) finance bridges troughs in cash flows and permits the company to weather transient periods of difficulty.

As a group, SMEs – compared to larger enterprises – often offer several advantages to a national economy, in so far as they are a major creator of jobs, an important source of innovation, versatile and flexible in response to market changes, and less susceptible to delocalization. They also provide a diffusion of economic decision-making power in society, with a likely positive effect on social stability, growth and progress. For an economy such as Italy (notably in the north of the country) at the start of the twenty-first century, 'a multitude of SMEs ... is a major source of strength: it means that Italy has proportionately more entrepreneurs and fewer employees than other countries, with the attendant benefits in terms of the liveliness of the economic and social fabric, the propensity to innovate and the diffusion of welfare' (Fortis and Carminati, 2007; also Calabrio and Carnazza, 2004).

Handicaps encountered by small businesses can be overcome through certain measures initiated by the private sector or public authorities. To illustrate, mechanisms of industry-wide collaboration among small enterprises could be envisaged in areas of infrastructure and expertise – by sharing costs and opportunities. (see, for example, *The Economist*, 2005b). Co-operation in infrastructure investments (for example, in 'information technology'), and in research and development programmes can be carried out collectively, to reduce costs and increase the benefits of small size.

Certain empirical studies have nevertheless shown that growth is influenced primarily by the quality of the business environment of the economy concerned, regardless of the size of its enterprises (according to the World Bank). The business environment is deemed to be attractive if:

(a) property rights are well protected;
(b) entry and exit barriers are relatively low;
(c) business registration and contract enforcement are not expensive;
(d) financial and other resources are readily accessible; and
(e) the insolvency process is efficient; that is, rapid and not onerous (see www.doingbusiness.org).

Large entrepreneurial businesses

Compared to SMEs, mature, large and established businesses – because of their accumulated know-how and capital resources or their sizeable predictable cash flows – can more easily access capital to invest in new areas that enable them to remain at the cutting-edge of competition, and to exploit business opportunities as they arise. Yet, several large listed enterprises are often pressured to produce profits over short-term horizons – sacrificing investment in profitable long-term projects in order to meet the next quarter's profit expectations announced to shareholders, investors and investment analysts or journalists.

One needs to reflect on the compatibility of *entrepreneurial spirit* with *big business*. The latter recruit *professional managers* who operate within an established organizational structure, and are guided by preset principles and rules. Managers are required to respect the enterprise's hierarchy and observe existing lines of authority and responsibility. Systems of delegation of responsibility, co-ordination among different units, and existing controls tend to be constraining for entrepreneurial innovators seeking flexibility to realize their projects.

In the highly competitive knowledge-based industries of the early twenty-first century, several established large or medium-sized enterprises have adopted explicit policies of fostering within their organizations a culture of innovation. This can be realized by giving their talented employees the opportunity and autonomy to think up, elaborate and develop their projects. The projects should be of strategic interest to the enterprise. With adequate resources to support them and financial incentives to reward their success, these employees are chosen for their scientific–technological know-how, their capacity to think and create 'outside conventional boxes', and their understanding of the markets in which they plan to sell their created products. This is notably the case with the global German industrial group Siemens, as outlined by the head of its technology and innovation division, Hermann Requardt (Requardt, 2007).

To avoid red tape, the entrepreneurial projects need to benefit from a degree of flexibility as warranted by changing conditions. A direct link between those principally involved in these entrepreneurial projects and top management helps to avoid undue delays resulting from hierarchies or red tape. Indeed, through that direct linkage with top management, the group responsible for innovation could thus avoid rigid controls (in planning, budgeting, reviews, and so on) when creativity necessitates a measure of deviation from preset rules or norms.

The challenge for entrepreneurial activities within large enterprises is that developers of innovative projects can disturb existing activities and may generate resistance from managers who are loath to see innovative projects perturb their well-oiled routine (see Basso and Pélisson, 2004). To remedy this constraint, it will be useful not to isolate the group responsible for innovation from related business activities within the large firm. The interaction of the two parties is bound to improve the quality of the innovative project and to enhance its acceptability by those involved in current activities. One may even advise that the employees/managers involved in the current business should also be rewarded for their positive collaboration – such as advising or facilitating the entry of new products. Otherwise, there would be risks of blockages, stonewalling, tensions and deadlocks arising from those busy with current business (see Kanter, 2006).

To address the constraints on the entrepreneurial culture within a large structured enterprise, and maintain the enterprise's position at the cutting edge of competitiveness, any of the following three strategies can prove productive – depending on the business environment. The first consists of resorting to the acquisition of, or partnership with, entrepreneurial start-ups that have developed innovations of proven value. The second calls for externalizing or spinning-off certain hitherto internal operations or services into independent companies (to be led by talented persons), and dealing with them at arm's length. The third fosters entrepreneurial activities within an efficiently organized large group under the aegis of top management. This approach will succeed if innovative entrepreneurial talents obtain human and material resources and autonomy in their work, in order to maximize value creation in accordance with the group's long-term objectives (see, for example, the works on large US corporations of business historian Alfred D. Chandler, notably his book *Strategy and Structure* [Chandler, 1975]; also Le Blanc, 2005).

Defining benefits

One could use two definitions for the performance of enterprises: (i) a *narrow* definition focuses on financial returns to owners or shareholders; and (ii) a *comprehensive* definition covers benefits derived by a wide spectrum of stakeholders. In the comprehensive version, stakeholders include owners, shareholders, investors, lenders, executives and management, employees, customers, suppliers, subcontractors, partners, various intermediaries, and the local or national community. An enterprise's contribution to a given community or the national economy is likely to be positively enhanced if its stakeholders' interests are reasonably satisfied (further developed in Chapter 5).

Those who own businesses generally stress the objective of 'shareholder value', while managers and employees focus on their compensation packages, the advancement in their careers, and their tenure. 'Proportionality' of benefits among stakeholders of an enterprise – though difficult to calibrate, attain and/or maintain – is a worthy objective to seek in order to promote the 'wealth creation' motivation of all parties concerned over the long term.

An enterprise's drive for the satisfaction of consumers and users is bound to generate benefits for shareholders and other stakeholders. As expressed by a seasoned business analyst, 'it may be more accurate, more motivating – and indeed more beneficial to shareholder value over the long term – to describe the ultimate purpose of business as the efficient provision of goods and services that society wants' (Ian Davis, worldwide managing director of McKinsey & Co.: Davis, 2005).

Beside shareholders and managers, the other stakeholders of an enterprise aspire to a treatment (material and non-material) perceived to be 'balanced' or 'fair'. It is thus vital to maintain cohesion, synergy and drive among all those involved in an enterprise – in order to sustain wealth creation for fair distribution among all parties concerned. Empirical evidence has shown that executives who embrace 'process fairness' reduce discontent, improve efficiency, generate support for new strategic initiatives, and promote an environment of creativity – thereby enhancing the enterprise's performance. This process comprises objective factors (participation in the wealth generated) and subjective factors (such as respect and recognition) that weigh importantly in a durable progress of an enterprise. Practising 'process fairness' successfully among stakeholders is a fine attribute of business leadership (see, for example, Brockner, 2006).

The impact of entrepreneurial activities is not confined to the stakeholders of the enterprises concerned. It can spill over to other enterprises and eventually to society at large. For example, a positive impact can lead to enhanced efficiency and growth in the economy (Phelps, 2005). Several sources (policy-makers, business leaders, academics) extol the significant role of SMEs in generating benefits through innovation, job creation, contribution to GDP, the spreading of wealth and the reduction of poverty (see, for example, IBM, 2006b;

also the International Finance Corporation, 'IFC SME Ventures Fund' at: www.ifc.org; Vandenberg, 2006; and van Stel *et al.*, 2004).

Recognizing the contribution of entrepreneurial SMEs to growth, governmental institutions (national or international) offer them financial support through private equity (PE) funds. Thus the intergovernmental International Finance Corporation (IFC) has invested in about 100 PE funds which have together invested (along with local interests) in over 1,000 companies in the developing world (see IFC, 2004). The UK government-owned PE fund of funds CDC Group plc, with net assets of US$4 billion committed to 100 PE funds, similarly focuses on SMEs in emerging markets. CDC's average annual return over 2003–7 reached 27 per cent (see CDC Group plc, 2007; available at: www.cdcgroup.com).

Entrepreneurs and market dynamics

The Austrian-American economist, Joseph Alois Schumpeter (1883–1950) had emphasized the role of innovative entrepreneurs as effective agents of change through their 'creative destruction' (see Schumpeter, 1942; also McCraw, 2007). He defines this phenomenon as the process leading to the eviction of established enterprises by budding entrepreneurial firms, whose new technologies, innovative products or new managerial approaches (by comparison to those of established enterprises) present a *superior appeal* to customers. Unable to sustain their sales, failing firms discontinue their activities and disband their workforce. The foregoing scenario can, nevertheless, be qualified with the following five considerations:

(i) A newly created product need not necessarily replace or destroy another product: it can add to the array of existing products. The new product will then cater for the unmet or expanding demands of consumers or users. Markets for new products could be created to satisfy new expanding wants, thus enlarging the supply of goods and services without necessarily displacing markets for existing products. Thus aeroplanes have not reduced the demand for cars, and new drugs have offered cures for untreated ills (see, for example, Bhidé, 2004).

(ii) The entry of new products is not determined solely by technological innovation (as measured by patents, spending on research and development, the creation of start-ups, or investments in venture capital). A 'new' product, notably in the consumer sector, can displace others for reasons not related to technological progress. This can be the case under conditions of changes in consumers' tastes in response to fashion, design, appeal, contagious passion to imitate others and so on.

(iii) The 'creation' of new enterprises with innovative products need not lead to the ineluctable total 'destruction' of established enterprises. The latter can be subject to metamorphoses. Assuming they have capable leaders, enterprises can be transmuted or renovated by reorganizing the use of their resources (material or non-material). They, in effect, re-invent themselves and ensure their survival by re-orientating or building on their existing activities – to enable them to serve the evolving needs of consumers or users more efficiently. Their existence as 'going concerns' can thus be maintained over long periods, while their activities are being transformed through weeding out unprofitable operations, streamlining, restructuring, and re-orientating their strategies.

(iv) Enterprises (or some of their units) can exit from a given market for reasons other than technological innovation. This is notably the case when barriers to trade or market inefficiencies are reduced or eliminated. Indeed, the enlargement of markets by the lifting of trade barriers among national economies is bound to lead to the delocalization of enterprises or their units of production from high-cost markets (notably mature developed economies) to lower-cost ones (such as emerging economies). This could then release labour and capital for deployment in new entrepreneurial activities aimed at efficiency gains and new products, and could over the medium term stem the decline in employment in the economies faced with the delocalization of established enterprises. Efficiency gains are likely to stimulate demand and would also allow for a reduction in work time for employed individuals, thus favouring leisure time.

(v) For enterprises that are not subject to rescue or transformation, remedies or palliatives can be put to work to ease the impact of socio-economic disturbances. These measures can take the form of appropriate incentives to recycle redundant workers of declining or failed enterprises to other appropriate jobs (on a full-time or part-time basis) within prosperous business sectors, adapting or re-training workers in new skills, and encouraging career flexibility and mobility of labour towards other regions and sectors thanks to appropriate incentives. By moderating disruption costs to society associated with economic transformations or turbulences, safety nets for dispensing temporary 'unemployment benefits' should help in cushioning economic downturns and smoothing transitions. Legislation and regulations have naturally to guard against the potentially pernicious effects of certain types of safety nets which might push some unemployed people into despondency, encouraging them to continue to draw welfare benefits from the 'nanny state' rather than venture into new activities or seek gainful employment.

Economic crises – accompanied by sharp falls in the level of economic activity and employment, and the closure of many enterprises – are not without eventual potential gains. From the vantage position

Exhibit 1.3 Determinants of geographical market expansion

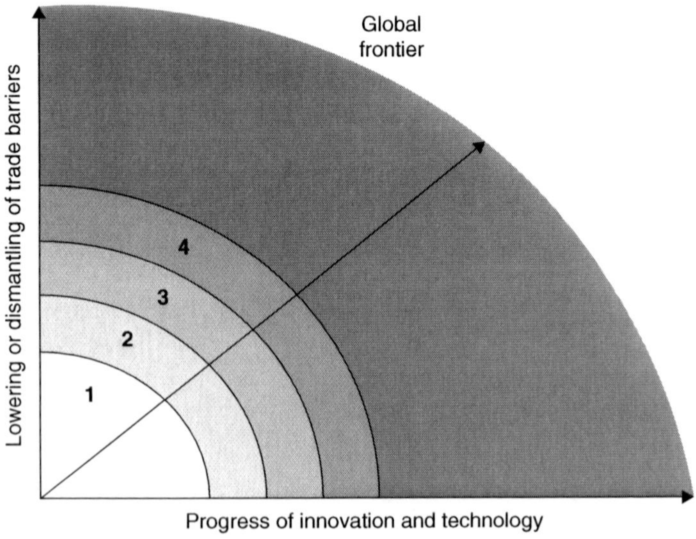

of an informed regulator, such crises might provide 'fertile ground for innovation and entrepreneurship', as evidenced by those that hit the Nordic countries (Norway, Sweden, Denmark and Finland) in the 1980s and 1990s (see Gjedrem, 2007).

New products and processes have been introduced to markets at a faster pace in recent decades, and innovative products have become accessible worldwide. Life cycles of new products have shortened. Markets have become characteristically dynamic with entry and/or exit of business units from markets becoming more frequent (see, for example, *The Economist*, 2007e). Exhibit 1.3 shows graphically that the competitive economic space is likely to expand from a local market to the global one with: (a) the lowering or dismantling of barriers imposed by governments or business groups; and/or (b) technological factors that reduce costs (of production, transport and others).

References

Association des Villageois de Ndem (2001) *Le village Ndem et son entreprise d'artisanat*, March.

Audrain, Xavier (2002) *Bay-Fall du Temps Mondial: Individus Modernes du Sénégal*, Master's thesis in African Studies, University of Paris I – Sorbonne.

Badaracco, Joseph L., (2006) 'Leadership in Literature', *Harvard Business Review*, Boston, Mass., March 2006, pp. 129–38.

Basso, Olivier and Pélisson, Gilles (2004) *Entrepreneurial Dynamics in Large Groups* (Paris: Institut de l'entreprise), December.

Bhidé, Amar (2004) 'More, Bigger, Faster', *The Conference Board Review*, September/October.

Bloomberg Markets (2007) 'Ethanol's Toxic Brew', *Bloomberg Markets*, October, p. 15.

Bosma, Niels, Jones, Kent, Autio, Erkko and Levie, Jonathan (2008) *GEM 2007 Executive Report*, sponsored by Babson College and London Business School.

Brockner, Joel (2006) 'Why It's So Hard to Be Fair', *Harvard Business Review*, March, pp. 122–9.

Calabrio, Marco and Carnazza, Paolo (2004) 'The Role and Strategies of Small and Micro Firms in Italy', *Review of Economic Conditions in Italy*, Rome, Capitalia, no. 3, pp. 465–92.

CDC Group plc (2007) *Annual Review 2007*.

Centre for Entrepreneurial and Financial Studies, Technische Universität München (2005) *Employment Contribution of Private Equity and Venture Capital in Europe*, EVCA (European Private Equity & Venture Capital Association), November.

Chandler, Alfred D. (1975) *Strategy and Structure* (Cambridge, Mass: MIT Press).

Christensen, Clayton M. and Raynor, Michael E. (2003) *The Innovator's Solution: Creating and Sustaining Successful Growth* (Boston, Mass.: Harvard Business School Press).

CompartamosBanco (2008) *A Letter to our Peers* by Carlos Danel and Carlos Labarthe, 17 June.

Daru, Patrick, Churchill, Craig and Beemsterboer, Erik (2003) *The Prevention of Debt Bondage with Microfinance-led Services* (Geneva: International Labour Office – ILO).

Davis, Ian (2005) 'What Is the Business of Business?', *The McKinsey Quarterly*, no. 3, pp. 105–13.

Dellien, Hans, Burnett, Jill, Gincherman, Anna and Lynch, Elizabeth (2005) *Product Diversification in Microfinance: Introducing Individual Lending* (New York: Women's World Banking), p. 8.

Delorme, Vincent (2005) *Perception des villageois de Ndem de leur project de développement, Sénégal* (Geneva: bachelor dissertation at Institute of Social Studies).

Deutsch, Klaus (2008) *Cap and Trade in America – US Climate Policy at a Crossroads* (Frankfurt am Main: Deutsche Bank Research), 5 May.

Dia, Demba Silèye (2000) 'Habiller: les artisans de Ndem au Sénégal – Ndem/Design: rencontre Art-Artisanat – La recherche de la perfection' ('Dressing: The Artisans of Ndem in Senegal – Ndem/Design: Meeting of Art-Craft – The Pursuit of Perfection'), *Le Journal*, Dakar.

Dicko, Oumar Hamadoun (2006) *General Assembly Opens Debate on International Migration*, New York, United Nations, 14 September, GA/10494, p. 2.

Dieckmann, Raimar (2007) *Microfinance: An Emerging Investment Opportunity – Uniting Social Investment and Financial Returns* (Frankfurt am Main: Deutsche Bank Research), 19 December.

Dodd, Randall (2007) 'Subprime: Tentacles of a Crisis', *Finance & Development*, IMF, December, pp. 15–19.

Drucker, Peter Ferdinand (1985) *Innovation and Entrepreneurship: Practice and Principles* (New York: Harper & Row).

Economist, The (2004) 'Passing on the Crown', 6 November, pp. 73–5.

Economist, The (2005a) 'The Hidden Wealth of the Poor', 3 November.

Economist, The (2005b) 'Financing German Companies – The Loan Factory', 16 April, p. 70.

Economist, The (2006a) 'Microcredit in India – Microsharks', 19 August, p. 58.

Economist, The (2006b) 'Europe's Senegal Connection – Faith in the Market', 23 December, pp. 97–8.

Economist, The (2007a) 'Agricultural Commodities – Biofuelled' (pp. 82–3) and 'A New Biofuel Made from Fruit Sugars' (p. 89), 23 June.

Economist, The (2007b) 'Mortgage-industry Lawsuits – the Finger of Suspicion', 22 December, pp. 111–12.

Economist, The (2007c) 'Something New Under the Sun – A Special Report on Innovation', 13 October.

Economist, The (2008a) 'Debt Relief – Waiving, not Drowning', 5 July, p. 80.

Economist, The (2008b) 'Microfinance – Poor People, Rich Returns', 17 May, p. 87.
Economist, The (2008c) 'Microfinance – Doing Good by Doing Very Nicely Indeed', 28 June, p. 20.
Economist, The (2009) 'Global heroes – A special report on entrepreneurship', 14 March.
Economist Technology Quarterly, The (2006) 'The Edison of Our Age?', 2 December, pp. 27–8.
Economist Technology Quarterly, The (2008) 'In Search of the Perfect Battery', 8 March, pp. 22–5.
Ellis, Luci (2008) *The Housing Meltdown: Why Did It Happen in the United States?*, BIS Working Papers, Monetary and Economic Department, September.
Etwareea, Ram (2008) 'Nobel Peace Laureate and Multi-entrepreneur', *Le Temps* newspaper, 27 September, p. 30.
European Commission (2003) *The New SME Definition – User Guide and Model Declaration*, May.
Felton, Andrew and Reinhart, Carmen M. (eds) (2008) *The First Global Financial Crisis of the 21st Century* (London: VoxEU/CEPR), June.
Fender, Ingo and Hördahl, Peter (2007) 'Overview: Markets Hit by Renewed Credit Woes', *BIS Quarterly Review*, December, pp. 1–17.
Fialka, John J. (2006) 'After Decades, A Solar Pioneer Sees Spark in Sales', *The Wall Street Journal*, 27 November.
Fortis, Mario and Carminati, Monica (2007) 'Industrial Districts: The Economic Reality and Legislative Framework in Italy', *Review of Economic Conditions in Italy*, January–April, Rome: Capitalia, pp. 9–40.
Gatti, Fabrizio (2008) *Bilal: mon voyage d'infiltré dans le monde des nouveaux esclaves* [*Bilal: My Trip as an Infiltrator in the World of the New Slaves*] (Paris: Liana Levi), May.
George, Bill, Sims, Peter, McLean, Andrew N. and Mayer, Diana (2007) 'Discovering Your Authentic Leadership', *Harvard Business Review*, Boston, Mass., February, pp. 47–55.
Gjedrem, Svein (Governor of Norges Bank) (2007), 'Economic Perspectives', *Economic Bulletin*, Oslo, April, pp. 4–14.
Global Entrepreneurship Monitor (GEM) Reports can be found at www.gemconsortium.org
Hirsch, Tim (2007) 'Project Aims to Extract Dam Methane', BBC News, 10 May.
IBM (2006a) *The Global CEO Study 2006* (Somers, NY: IBM Global Services).
IBM (2006b), *Global Innovation Outlook 2.0* (Somers, NY: IBM Global Services) March.
IFC (International Finance Corporation) (2004) *2004 Annual Review: Small Business Activities* (Washington DC: World Bank Group), p. 10.
Jallow, Katharina (1996) 'Miracles and Mysticisms', *Djembe* magazine, no. 16, April.
Kanter, Rosabeth Moss (2006) 'Innovation: The Classic Traps', *Harvard Business Review*, November, pp. 72–83.

Kota, Ina (2007) 'Microfinance for the Poor', *Finance and Development*, IMF, June, pp. 44–5.
Kridel, Tim (2006) 'Meet Stan Ovshinsky, the Energy Genius', *Mother Earth News*, October–November.
Labarthe, Gilles (2008) 'Le mouridisme, un défi aux theories du développement?', Agence de presse DATAS, Summer 2008: www.datas.ch/article.php?id=552
La Torre, Mario and Vento, Gianfranco A. (2006) *Microfinance* (Basingstoke: Palgrave Macmillan).
Le Blanc, Gilles (2005) *L'industrie dans l'économie française (1978–2003): une analyse comparative* ... (*Industry in the French Economy (1978–2003): A Comparative Analysis* ...) (Paris: Institut de l'entreprise), April.
Le Monde newspaper (2006) 17–18 December, p. 19.
Linnermann, Carsten (2007) *Germany's Mittelstand – An Endangered Species?*, (Frankfurt am Main: Deutsche Bank Research), 6 July.
Lunnon, Jenny (2007) 'Nothing Ventured, Nothing Gained', *Oxford Today*, Hilary issue, pp. 30–1.
Macartney, Jane (2007) 'Three Gorges Dam is a Disaster in the Making, China Admits', *The Times*, 27 September.
McCraw, Thomas K. (2007) *Prophet of Innovation: Joseph Schumpeter and Creative Destruction* (Cambridge, Mass.: The Belknap Press of Harvard University Press).
Meyer, Thomas (2007) *Venture Capital in Europe — Spice for European Economies*, (Frankfurt am Main: Deutsche Bank Research), 2 October.
Meyer, Thomas (2008) *Venture Capital: Bridge between Idea and Innovation?*, (Frankfurt am Main: Deutsche Bank Research), 9 May.
Naffziger, D. W., Avila, R. A. and Avila, S. M. (1999) '*Transition Funding in Family Firms*' (Muncie, Ind.: Ball State University).
Norges Bank (2005) *Financial Stability*, No. 2/2005 (Oslo: Norges Bank), 23 May, pp. 19–24.
Norges Bank (2007) 'Problems in the US Residential Mortgage Market', *Financial Stability* (Oslo: Norges Bank), December, pp. 42–4.
OECD (Organisation for Economic Co-operation and Development) and FAO (Food and Agricultural Organization of the United Nations) (2007), *OECD–FAO Agricultural Outlook 2007–2016* (Paris: OECD/FAO), July.
OECD (Organisation for Economic Co-operation and Development) (2008) *OECD Environmental Outlook to 2030* (Paris: OECD).
Phelps, Edmund S. (2006) *Macroeconomics for a Modern Economy*, Economics Nobel Prize Lecture, 8 December.
Porter, Michael E. (1998) *Competitive Strategy – Techniques for Analyzing Industries and Competitors* (New York: Simon & Schuster).
Porter, Michael E. and Kramer, Mark R. (2006) 'Strategy and Society: The Link Between Competitive Advantage and Corporate Social Responsibility', *Harvard Business Review*, December, pp. 78–92.
Refugee Studies Centre (2006–7), *Annual Report 2006–2007*, Department of International Development, University of Oxford.

Requardt, Hermann (2007) 'My Inventors Are the Entrepreneurs of Their Own Ideas' (in French), *L'Usine Nouvelle*, 13 September, Paris, pp. 10–12,

Roy, Michael (1998) 'By Toil, Transpiration and Solidarity, Water Flows at Ndem' (in French), *Le Courrier*, Geneva newspaper, 13 September.

Schumpeter, Joseph Alois (1942) *Capitalism, Socialism and Democracy* (New York: Harper & Brothers)[5th edn London: George Allen & Unwin, 1976].

Skelton, Rose (2006) *Spiritual Work Bears Fruit in Senegal*, BBC News, 20 June.

Srivastava, Ravi S. (2005) *Bonded Labour in India – Its Incidence and Pattern* (Geneva: International Labour Office – ILO), June.

Tyler, Richard (2008) 'PM Launches School for Tycoons', *Daily Telegraph*, 11 March, p. B2.

UN Conference on Climate Change (2007) *The Future in Our Hands: Addressing the Leadership Challenge of Climate Change*, New York, 24 September.

United Nations Conference on Trade and Development (2009) *The Global Economic Crisis: Systemic Failures and Multilateral Remedies*, New York and Geneva, 65pp.

US Securities and Exchange Commission, Energy Conversion Devices, Inc. (2007) Form 10-Q, filed 8 February.

Vandenberg, Paul (2006) *Poverty Reduction Through Small Enterprises*, Working paper, International Labour Office, Geneva.

van Doorn, Judith and Churchill, Craig (2004) *Microfinance Against Child Labour – Technical Guidelines* (Geneva: International Labour Organization), February.

van Stel, André, Carree, Martin and Thurik, Roy (2004) *The Effect of Entrepreneurship on National Economic Growth: An Analysis Using the GEM Database*, Scientific Analysis of Entrepreneurship and SMEs, Paper N200320, Berlin, April.

Villiger, Maggie (2004) 'Meet the Ovshinskys', *Scientific American Frontiers*, 19 May.

Vogel, Frank E. and Hayes, Samuel L. III (1998) *Islamic Law and Finance: Religion, Risk, and Return* (The Hague/Boston, Mass.: Kluwer Law International).

Wall Street Journal Europe (2006) 'Macro Microfinance', 20 November.

Yee, Amy (2008) 'The Founding Family's Sale of Ranbaxy to Daïchi Takes the Company to Another Level of Business – Big Pharma Meets Generics', *Financial Times*, 16 June, p.16.

Yellen, Janet L., President and CEO of the Federal Reserve Bank of San Francisco (2008), 'Opening Remarks to the 2008 National Interagency Community Reinvestment Conference', 31 March.

Yunus, Muhammad and Grameen Bank (2009) *Grameen Bank at a Glance*, September; available at: www.grameen-info.org.

Part 2
Financiers as Business Developers

Entrepreneurial talents span several fields of human endeavour. Part 2 focuses on entrepreneurial talents in the private equity (PE) sector. PE entrepreneurs mobilize and deploy 'risk capital' and managerial/technical know-how through investment funds: their objective is to own or control promising companies and to create value therefrom. By nurturing these companies' activities over set time horizons, they expect to generate benefits for themselves and for their investors, and eventually for other stakeholders. The following analysis attempts an evaluation of strategies and practices used by these entrepreneurs, by reference to stakeholders' benefits and societal progress.

2

Diversity of Entrepreneurial Financiers

This chapter reviews (a) potential sources of funding available to entrepreneurial projects and to growth businesses; (b) major factors that have contributed to the growth of *private* capital vehicles for business development; and (c) strategies that guide business developers in acquiring businesses, and eventually selling them at higher value.

Sources of entrepreneurial capital

Entrepreneurs' initial resources

Seed capital of entrepreneurial businesses is largely provided by the entrepreneurs themselves, at the start of their activities. One study shows that entrepreneurs provided 65.8 per cent of the start-up capital for their new ventures in 2004, in thirty-four countries – as analysed by Bygrave and Hunt (2005). One could deduce from this statistical finding that a better environment for breeding and developing entrepreneurship exists in an economy which:

(a) generates wealth and savings for significant investments in promising novel business opportunities;
(b) enjoys a higher standard of living and education reasonably diffused among various layers of society; and
(c) has a business-friendly environment that encourages – *inter alia* – a culture of free thinking and creativity.

Among the multitude of small businesses, start-ups with technological ambitions are foremost in entrepreneurial activities in the

21st century. They typically need risk capital to improve their opportunity of developing their innovations which could require a comparatively long time horizon.

Non-institutional providers of risk capital are of two kinds: (a) family members and friends; or (b) wealthy third parties (unrelated to the entrepreneurs) who are willing to gamble on the entrepreneurs' ideas, in the hope of 'hitting the jackpot' (known as *business angels*). In addition to capital, business angels contribute their seasoned technical advice, managerial expertise and business savvy derived from previous personal experiences at the helm of various enterprises (see, for example, Colin M. Mason in Parker, 2006).

A variety of reasons prompt a founding owner-manager of an enterprise to seek financial partners by selling (totally or partially) to outsiders his/her property rights. Chief among these reasons are one or more of the following:

(i) the wish of a founding entrepreneur to give her/his business the best possible opportunity for future growth, and thus perpetuate its activities or its vocation;
(ii) the absence of competent and willing successors from within the family circle of an ageing founder;
(iii) the founder's opportunity to cash-in on achievements through the sale of his/her enterprise (or a significant portion of it) in order to carry out other activities; or
(iv) the absence of debt financing from financial intermediaries at reasonable terms.

Unforeseen managerial problems could also lead to the sale of a family business's (FB's) value. These could include unexpected conflicts between an owner-manager and his personnel, or a dire personal situation – such as a crippling injury, chronic sickness, divorce or death. Such situations would drive owner-managers to dispose abruptly of their ownership at knockdown prices. Personal emergencies and organizational/operational troubles are potentially acute in FBs and other SMEs. Consequently, an owner-manager of a business stands to gain from the foresight of distinguishing between running a business efficiently, and family affairs. In the absence of family succession, a well-prepared voluntary transfer of ownership and management to qualified internal professionals (a management buyout – MBO) or an orderly sale to outsiders (such as a management buy-in – MBI) should enhance the value of the enterprise and be the least disruptive to stakeholders. Given the familiarity of internal managers with the business, an MBO is generally less risky than an MBI – other things remaining equal. In both MBO and MBI, institutional capital providers can take a significant role – as discussed below.

Institutional capital providers

Institutional capital providers focusing on start-up entrepreneurial firms – referred to as venture capital (VC) funds – may seek a majority or a minority interest, depending on particular circumstances and opportunities. Thus, a VC fund can be well-advised to opt for a minority interest in investee entrepreneurial firms, for two reasons (i) to sustain the entrepreneurs' drive for creativity (as entrepreneurs are highly motivated by the feeling that they are working for their *own* enterprises); and/or (ii) to spread risks across a much larger number of business units for a given size of an investment fund (than would otherwise be the case in majority ownership of companies).

Failure to find appropriate and sufficient finance on reasonable terms for a promising small enterprise could well jeopardize its future development and its capacity to grow. Owner-managers (and their circle of family and friends) may not have adequate personal resources to fund the expansion of their enterprises. Moreover, business angels may not be available. Finally, external debt financing by banking intermediaries may not be accessible, for a variety of reasons. Among these reasons, one could list

(a) conditions peculiar to the small firm (such as, for example, an insufficient equity base, a lack of bankable collaterals, and/or excessive opacity or dissimulation of important facts);
(b) the enterprise's high uncertainties or risks (e.g. with reference to its cash flows), and the banks' concern to moderate their own risks;
(c) the availability of safer lending opportunities for banks, namely with larger and more diversified business groups;
(d) inadequacies of the small firm's management;
(e) the existence of a general liquidity crunch; and/or
(f) various socio-economic constraints (see, for example, European Commission, 2003).

Institutional providers of capital resources to businesses are multifarious. They can be classified as follows:

(a) independent specialized groups which set up PE funds and solicit capital from various groups of investors;
(b) captive investment pools that belong to sizeable financial institutions – such as insurance companies, pension/retirement funds, commercial banks, investment or merchant banks, hedge funds and others;
(c) conglomerates such as Berkshire Hathaway and General Electric (GE) (see, for example, *Bloomberg Markets*, 2007);
(d) industrial or trading firms;
(e) affluent people or families operating through trust companies;
(f) foundations and endowments (of universities and others);
(g) hybrid, multi-purpose financial pools that leverage their existing client base; and
(h) state-owned investment vehicles, also referred to as 'sovereign-wealth funds', operating independently or investing through other financial groups (see, for example, IFSL Research, 2008b; available at: http://www.ifsl.org.uk).

Equity funds as *engines* of wealth creation can speed up the orderly expansion of the activities of promising companies starved of funding. They can also ensure the smooth transmission of skills, know-how, and business–human relations from a retiring generation of founding owner-managers to a new managerial generation of talented people who are given the opportunity to push further the frontier of creativity and profitability already attained by the founders. Among the declared main objectives of PE funds is that of taking over promising SMEs in order to prolong their cycle of 'wealth creation' beyond the active professional lifespan of the founding entrepreneur(s). Investors in these funds expect to reap in a few years substantial benefits upon the sale of their portfolios of investee companies, while the acquired firms and their stakeholders expect to gain from the PE funds' nurturing (in financial, managerial and/or industrial – technical support).

Financial firms – regardless of their organization or ownership – can manage, under one corporate roof, multiple 'pools of capital' (covering several types of PE funds with differentiated strategies, hedge funds, mutual funds, real-estate funds, senior debt funds, mezzanine funds and others) and provide multiple financial services.

Hedge funds are generally unregulated (or only lightly regulated) and have attracted large pools of capital since the 1980s seeking higher returns for their investors, admittedly at a higher risk compared to other investments. Unlike PE firms, they typically invest in marketable financial instruments to meet investors' redemptions. In more recent years, several hedge funds have created 'side pockets' (up to as much as 15 per cent of their total assets) for private illiquid investments. These are not redeemable until the sale of the investments, which may take a few years (Townley, 2006; see also Chapter 4).

In addition to mainstream 'direct PE funds', investors – small and large – have also shown a strong interest in PE 'funds of funds'. The latter refer to funds whose activities are limited to investing in other funds (whether on a discretionary or non-discretionary basis). These funds offer investors a wider scope to diversify, a higher degree of liquidity, smaller investment commitments and lesser risks for investors – compared to 'direct PE funds'. Funds of funds can also appeal to sizeable investors by offering them segregated accounts, managed to meet the investors' particular legal, tax, strategic or other requirements: this type of investor is often quite sophisticated and demanding with respect to information and performance (see Sovran, 2006; and Lai, 2005).

Among institutional investors that command stable and sizeable financial resources, one can refer to pension funds (privately-owned or state-owned/supported) and sovereign funds. Both can play an important role in funding potentially promising enterprises, and thus promoting growth and progress. Nevertheless, regulatory constraints in several countries confine the bulk of pension funds' investments to government bonds, government-insured bank deposits, and the shares of large 'blue chip' companies. Authorizing pension funds (even for a small portion of their large savings) to access PE-like investments in start-ups and micro/small companies is likely to invigorate economies (through the funding of large numbers of potentially creative entrepreneurs).

Sovereign-wealth funds (see Box 2.1) have been set up for a variety of national motives – which vary in importance from one country to another. Chief among these motives, one could mention:

(i) a long-term strategy of investing a portion of export proceeds in financial and non-financial assets that could sustain future generations once national resources are fully depleted or once they lose their commercial value;

(ii) cushioning eventual periods of economic downturn or socio-political crisis;

(iii) diversifying governmental reserves from traditional monetary reserves (foreign exchange and/or precious metals) to other classes of assets;

(iv) reallocating a portion of financial reserves away from countries that are deemed to be unstable or insecure for political/strategic or economic/financial reasons, to be invested in more stable economies and/or friendly countries;

(v) seeking to benefit from the expertise and managerial resources of foreign investee companies to develop their national economies; and/or

(vi) use their investments to raise their influence in host countries – although this last motive is likely in certain circumstances to be counter-productive (see, for example, 'The rise of state capitalism – Coming to grips with sovereign-wealth funds', *A special report on globalization – The Economist*, 20 September 2008, p. 17–19).

Innovators, pioneers and entrepreneurs exist in all walks of life, and extend to those responsible for governmental institutions. This is illustrated in Box 2.1 by reference to the creation of a sovereign wealth fund to invest the 'surplus' oil revenues of the State of Kuwait. The fund seeks to sustain the perennial existence of the state beyond the oil era (that is, after the depletion of oil resources or the loss of their commercial attractiveness). The financial vehicle in question, set up as a legal entity in 1950, has the responsibility of investing its allocated financial resources worldwide and accumulating wealth to meet the nation's eventual future shortfalls in income.

Sovereign funds' activities in host countries are likely to elicit general acceptance if certain conditions prevail. These comprise the existence of reciprocally open markets among investor–investee countries, the avoidance of politically-sensitive investments, and abiding by internationally-agreed best practices – such as transparency (see, for example, IMF, 2008; Kern, 2007; *The Economist*, 2007c; and Tassell and Chung, 2007). One could argue that sovereign funds are generally welcome in host countries encountering acute shortages of capital.

Banks: owners of non-financial enterprises or lenders?

In a few countries (such as in continental Europe), several banking groups in the nineteenth and twentieth centuries were organized as *universal banks*, effectively business conglomerates in so far as they owned and ran various non-financial businesses alongside their regular financial activities. In the absence of developed stock exchanges

Box 2.1 Kuwait's pioneering sovereign wealth fund as a global investor

Kuwait is a barren, arid land with scant underground sources of drinking water, located at the head of the Arabian–Persian Gulf. Its area extends over 17,820 square kilometres. Prior to the Second World War, Kuwait's small population – estimated at less than 50,000 in the early 1930s (compared with about 3 million in 2008, two-thirds of them expatriates) lived frugally, depending on shipbuilding (using wood imported from India), pearl diving, fishing and trade between the Indian subcontinent and the Arabian Gulf. In 1934, the Emir of Kuwait (Shaikh Ahmad Al-Jaber Al-Sabah) granted an on-shore oil concession covering the whole territory of the state (excluding the Neutral Zone territory, which falls under the joint sovereignty of Kuwait and Saudi Arabia) to the Anglo-American joint venture Kuwait Oil Company (KOC), owned equally by the Anglo-Persian Oil Company later renamed the British Petroleum Company (UK-owned) and the Gulf Oil Corporation (US-owned).

Well-advised, the succeeding Emir of Kuwait, Shaikh Abdullah Al-Salem Al-Sabah (1950–65) decided immediately on his accession to Kuwait's leadership to set up a fund for future generations (the Kuwait Investment Office – KIO) the very first such modern 'sovereign wealth fund' as acknowledged by the Deputy Governor of the Bank of England, Sir John Gieve (his speech on 'Sovereign wealth funds and global imbalances', to the Sovereign Wealth Management Conference in London, 14 March 2008). Operating out of London since the beginning of 1953, KIO's resources have been built with a portion of the oil revenues bonanza for deployment in lucrative investments internationally. The timing was propitious on the eve of the surge of oil revenues (as a result of the discovery of the giant Burgan oil field in Kuwait in the late 1930s, and its development shortly afterwards).

Kuwait's objectives in setting KIO were essentially four: (i) to avoid squandering its relatively large oil revenues that are beyond the absorptive capacity of the domestic economy; (ii) to avoid spendthrift practices that could sap or corrupt the citizens' work ethos; (iii) to diversify state revenues and compensate for an eventual drastic decline in oil revenues; and (iv) to demonstrate solidarity *vis-à-vis* future Kuwaiti generations by providing them with other productive resources for the post-oil era (that is, when oil reserves get depleted or lose their commercial attractiveness).

Contemporary Kuwaiti citizens have had the benefits of a welfare state that distributed its oil income generously through a variety of means: free education at all levels, free healthcare, retirement income, grants of land, marriage bonuses, subsidized housing loans (subject to debt relief), cash grants, virtually guaranteed employment, and other benefits. These benefits are not available to foreign residents.

Kuwait obtained its independence from Great Britain on 19 June 1961. The concessionary company was later (in 1976) acquired by the State of Kuwait.* In that year, a Reserve Fund for Future Generations (RFFG) was created, by transferring into it 50 per cent of the assets of the state of Kuwait's General Reserve Fund, 10 per cent of the regular state revenues, and all the investment income of the state. (RFFG and KIO later became part of the organizational structure of the state-owned Kuwait Investment Authority.) The oil windfall, partially transformed into income-producing foreign assets, serves to diversify the current income of the state from sole dependence on oil revenues. In 1986, government revenues from investments exceeded its revenues from oil. The assets are largely invested in developed and emerging economies, and are widely diversified geographically and sectorially. Investments include marketable securities of financial and non-financial companies, as well as equity stakes in major industrial or trading companies, real estate and property development ventures, and others.

The RFFG and KIO have been vital in periods of crisis. In particular, during Iraq's occupation of Kuwait from August 1990 to February 1991, critical funding was available from these investment pools to subsidize Kuwaiti families overseas, to defray the expenses of the Kuwait government in exile, to cover the costs of

Allied armies and their military operations in connection with the liberation of Kuwait, and to continue Kuwait's aid programmes towards friendly developing nations. Moreover, the rapid reconstruction of the Kuwait economy was made possible after the 1990–91 occupation that involved the destruction of property and the systematic burning of oil wells.

Note: *The author, in the capacity of Resident Adviser to the Kuwait Minister of Finance and Oil, was entrusted with studies leading to the acquisition of KOC's concessionary rights by the State of Kuwait, and participated actively in the relevant negotiations in Kuwait and the United Kingdom. Details on the international investments of the State of Kuwait can be accessed through the Kuwait Investment Authority and its related links: see http://www.kia.gov.kw.

capable of channelling investors' capital to companies in need of funding, universal banks had the resources to invest in these companies. These banks thus became large shareholders and partners of various companies they nurtured with capital, sustained with loans, and/or co-managed. Some of these firms later developed into large and eventually publicly-listed companies – with their partner banks continuing to hold significant equity stakes, and to provide them with funding and other financial services. The banks' stakes in the ownership of non-financial companies were recorded as 'permanent participations' in the banks' balance sheet. These stakes were not intended for sale, and constituted an important category of the banks' assets and income (see, for example, Mikdashi, 1998).

These banking groups have had a key role in nurturing enterprises, beginning with the modern industrial era (through various forms of equity or debt) over long time horizons. Several countries had espoused the model of universal banks with diversified activities spanning deposit-taking-cum-credit, brokerage, mergers and acquisitions (M&A), asset management, private equity, investment banking, stakes of ownership in non-financial businesses, among others. These ownership stakes could be sizeable and cover companies in various economic sectors – manufacturing, real estate, trading, services and others.

Higher capital adequacy requirements on banks' non-financial assets have been recommended by the Basel Committee on Banking

Supervision (BCBS) composed of regulators of major financial markets' jurisdictions (see http://www.bis.org). They became fully operational since 2007. Banks, in compliance with the exigencies of their national regulators, begun already in 2003 spinning-off or shedding from their balance sheets the direct or indirect ownership of captive industrial or commercial companies, along with other non-financial assets (see Chapter 4) – to avoid higher capital requirements in line with the higher risks of these assets in comparison with secured debt financing.

The broad scope of universal banks' activities can be a source of conflicts of interest. Thus, PE firms and their investors (such as pension funds) may decline to consider acquisition deals through an all-purpose bank if they fear that the bank is proposing a company of lower attractiveness to outsiders while keeping the better deals and more favourable terms for the bank's own PE affiliate. An independent PE firm would then be reluctant to call on these financial institutions for impartial advice, debt financing or underwriting, if they deem them to be direct rival investors in the PE sector – unless there are robust firewalls among the departments of the all-purpose bank.

Banks have nevertheless developed their lending activities to PE firms which resort to LBO (leveraged buyout) or the financing of the acquisition of a business unit using mostly debt. Some banks have also sought minority equity interests in non-financial enterprises or in PE funds (with ostensibly no involvement in the management of the investee companies concerned or no influence over their strategies) in order to avoid onerous capital requirements for majority interests as required by current regulations. Such minority interests offer the investing bank the opportunity to gain additional valuable insights into the businesses concerned, and to generate revenues from interest margins on loans, and various commissions or fees on a variety of financial services offered to the above-mentioned investee enterprises.

The genesis of the PE sector

The PE sector, and in particular its VC (venture capital) segment, was in gestation towards the beginning of the twentieth century. The VC fund concept came formally to fruition with the establishment in 1946 of the American Research and Development Corporation

(ARD) in Boston, USA, as the first publicly-owned and traded venture capital firm. Its conception and success are attributed largely to Georges Doriot (1899–1987), a French-born naturalized American (who had first embraced a military career and then became, after the Second World War, a professor at the Harvard Business School). ARD's objective was to revitalize the New England economy through technology-based industries, thus compensating for the demise of the garment and textile industry. ARD became the first profit-making US venture capital firm. Its aim was to appraise business opportunities, select investee companies for funding (in so-called 'sunrise' or technology-based industries) and monitor their performance (one of ARD's most successful investments has been Digital Equipment Corporation). ARD founders' vision was to replace the 'sunset' industries (such as leather goods and textiles) that were on the wane. As a pioneering organization aimed at investing in technology-driven start-up innovative firms in need of stable funds. ARD's founders and investors took some convincing that the future would bring them large gains along with the social reward of fulfilling their civic duties productively (see Hsu and Kenney, 2004).

In a similar way to ARD, a British company, the Industrial and Commercial Finance Corporation Limited (ICFC), was established in 1945, under the chairmanship of William Piercy (later Lord Piercy) by a syndicate of British joint stock banks and the Bank of England, to provide long and medium term finance to high-growth SMEs. Starting with £10 million to invest, ICFC (which was originally limited to the British market) – now 3i – has become the UK's biggest listed private equity group (covering buyouts, growth capital and venture capital) with a global reach and a market capitalization of Euro 6.5 billion in 2006. At the end of September 2007, it was managing £5.13 billion off its balance sheet, and £2.45 billion of third party funds (see www.3i.com; http://library-2.lse.ac.uk/archives/handlists/Piercy/m.html; also *Financial Times*, March 2008).

Since the mid-1940s, the PE sector has been growing considerably, measured by reference to its contribution to gross domestic product (GDP) in market economies, as shown by different industry studies. The growth has come mainly through the establishment of independent and specialized PE firms. PE firms have spurred the development of a network of supporting organizations which provide advice, identify opportunities and assist in executing transactions.

The sector has thus energized economies through enhancing the competitiveness of several enterprises.

Over the last quarter of the twentieth century and the first decade of the twenty-first, firms managing PE investments have moved from a *niche* situation in business finance to a central position in the capitalist system (see, for example, *The Economist*, 2004). PE firms manage funds that acquire significant ownership stakes (majority or minority) in privately-owned companies (that is, not listed on stock exchanges). The vast majority of investee companies belong to the category of SMEs. Outside the USA, the United Kingdom is the leading country in the PE field, with some 20 per cent of British business assets owned by PE firms in 2006 (see *Financial Times*, 2006; also British Venture Capital Association, 2006). Early in 2008, the UK IFSL (International Financial Services London) ranked, in US$ trillions, the assets of major categories of financial vehicles at the end of 2007 as follows: pension funds (28.5), mutual funds (27.3), insurance funds (19.1), sovereign wealth funds (3.3), hedge funds (1.9), and private equity (0.8) (IFSL Research, 2008a; available at: http://www.ifsl.org.uk/research; also Farrell and Lund 2008).

Principles and practices

PE vehicles have encompassed three main categories of investments: 'buyouts', 'venture capital' and 'turnarounds'. The first category – buyouts – generally applies to investments in established, mature or growth companies in need of transitional equity funding for further growth, or for facilitating the transfer of ownership. Buyout transactions have involved the purchase of family businesses (FBs) with no sibling able or willing to take over, and other SMEs. In the recent past, sizeable publicly traded companies have also been acquired by PE firms, and then converted into privately-owned companies.

The second category of PE investments – venture capital – concentrates on incubating or start-up companies. These investments concern mainly innovative companies at an early stage of their development, with a potential of generating high profits for investors – and admittedly subject to a higher degree of uncertainty regarding outcomes by comparison with buyouts.

The third category – turnarounds – deals with distressed companies that have the potential of returning to profitability once they have been rescued by hands-on competent management (through efficient reorganization, rationalization and streamlining of expenses, downsizing, re-orientation towards income-generating activities, closure of loss-making departments, and other strategies) underpinned by appropriate recapitalization (see Turnaround Management Association at: http://www.turnaround.org; also *The Economist*, 2007b). In turnaround situations, a PE firm gets intensively involved with investee ailing companies. PE managers need to have the wise judgement and the force of character to take painful decisions to close unproductive units and dismiss redundant personnel. This could also call for facing up to trade unions' industrial actions, local communities' protests or governmental pressures in order to revitalize the companies concerned and put them on the path to long-term growth.

A PE firm usually manages one or more pools of capital with the objective of acquiring equity stakes in non-listed or de-listed companies. Its main functions centre on two areas. The first category of functions consist of tapping financial institutions and high net worth people with abundant capital resources for medium-/long-term investments. With such investors, the PE firm is not subject to 'earning myopia' of reporting regularly (often on a quarterly basis) positive results, as demanded by public shareholders and financial analysts of publicly listed companies. The second category of functions consist of providing seasoned advice, networking and know-how in the managerial and technical fields to investee companies to increase their value before exit (as expounded in Chapter 3).

Performing PE firms, acting as efficient *agents* on behalf of investors, share a few intertwined strategic features. Their management (a) is endowed with polyvalent complementary managerial talents, combining both financial and industrial expertise capable of providing net added value to targeted companies; (b) has the capacity of mobilizing financial resources from investors (the *principal*) for medium-/long-term productive investments by PE managers (the *agent*); and (c) is strongly financially motivated to pursue relentlessly and proactively managerial oversight and effective help to investee companies aimed at generating substantial *net value* until exit.

To launch PE funds, mainstream teams of PE managers prospect high net worth individuals or institutional investors. Investors may not exceed 100 participants for a given fund and agree to commit capital (generally a large sum) over an agreed time horizon. They accept the relatively high risk of illiquid PE investments to be made in a limited number of enterprises in the expectation of superior returns – by comparison with publicly traded liquid securities (a liquid market is defined as an efficient, transparent and sizeable one, in which the average single investor can readily buy or sell securities with minimal transaction costs and without altering market prices).

Investors turning to a PE firm operating several non-listed funds might be confronted by certain challenges. One of these concerns their ability to choose the investment fund that serves their investment strategy and interests optimally. Another challenge is to ensure that inter-fund transactions – if any – are conducted at 'fair value'. More generally, it is important to ascertain that the legitimate rights of investors are not damaged insidiously. One could reasonably assume that big investors – compared to smaller ones – have easier access to information from PE firms.

The hypothesis that PE firms seek the long term development of investee companies effectively and consistently has been questioned in certain quarters. A few critics invoke cases where PE firms have sought financial returns or 'squeezing value' out of business acquisitions in the short term in lieu of 'adding value' through longer-term development. Certain critics have likened PE firms to leeches, akin to *corporate raiders* driven by a 'pillaging instinct', and interested primarily in the take-over of undervalued companies in order to sell them soon afterwards with no real contribution being made by the concerned PE firms. The sale can be realized after (i) installing a new management; and/or (ii) dismantling, or spinning-off, one or more divisions of the acquired company. The objective of these PE firms – according to critics – is to obtain prompt gains by reselling the acquired companies within a short period of time, rather than by nurturing their growth for the benefit of stakeholders over the long term (see *The Economist*, 2005a and 2005b).

Trade unions, in particular, argue generally that 'the planning horizon [of PE firms] is becoming shorter and shorter, and shareholder value and returns on owners' investments are prioritized above anything else, even real economic performance ... [which] is obviously a threat to sustainable enterprise development in the form of research, development and innovation'. Moreover, labour representatives claim that the loyalty of top executives of publicly listed companies shifts from their own shareholders and employees to PE funds, to the extent that these executives are enticed with high compensation packages if they agree to the take-over – while not disclosing to the public such salary arrangements which become a 'private' affair (see International Trade Union Confederation, 2007; also UNI Global Union, 2007). The fairer sharing of risks and rewards among stakeholders, as advocated by labour unions, instils in workers a strong motivation to increase the 'value pie'. The challenge remains the definition of a 'fair' split. Workers' sharing in risks implies that they are ready in periods of economic downturn to contain their wage claims or even to accept being laid off temporarily in the expectation of an upturn in economic activities in the near future. To facilitate this process, the unemployed should, it is hoped, be eligible for appropriate compensatory measures (safety nets) provided by the company or the authorities concerned. The same reasoning should apply to management's compensation packages.

Although privately owned companies do not disclose detailed information on their activities, their key stakeholders (customers, suppliers and employees) have 'a legitimate interest in the health of a business' (see Lambert, 2007). In particular, trade unions claim that some PE firms lack transparency and use investee companies as *cash cows*. They would thus load them with too much debt to obtain (i) a fiscal shield (consisting of lower taxable income after deducting debt charges) to reduce corporate tax payments; (ii) to extract a variety of fees, pre-paid *carried interest* (also referred to as *carry*), and other benefits; and (iii) benefit from tax exemptions on the *carry* (see, for example, Service Employees International Union, 2008; available at: http://www.seiu.org).

The model of progress-driven entrepreneurial financiers, prompted by the objective of nurturing investee companies over the medium term for the benefit of all stakeholders, has not proved invariably realistic for the PE sector. To illustrate, one can refer to an episode by a leading US-based PE firm, Blackstone, which bought Celanese AG in 2004 for US$650 million. The company's largest shareholder (Kuwait Petroleum Company, with 29 per cent of the shares) was comforted by the so-called 'fairness opinion' of Blackstone's investment bank, Goldman Sachs, which netted US$21 million in fees for the sale. Blackstone de-listed Celanese from the Frankfurt stock exchange. Nine months later, it took the same investee company public on the New York stock exchange. The new listing yielded Blackstone's PE fund some US$3 billion (in addition to shares it had held on to), and its investment banker also received substantial (undisclosed) fees. This opportunistic PE operation does not reflect the *nurturing* strategy over the medium term claimed by most PE funds. Blackstone reportedly 'took US$45 million from Celanese Corp for its advisory work on its own deal in 2004, more than twice the US$18 million Celanese paid Goldman Sachs' (see the Blackstone Group, 2003; and Weinberg and Vardi, 2006).

Some PE firms' quick-money mindset has been documented. This was, for example, the case of Thomas H. Lee Partners which, three weeks after buying an 80 per cent stake of Iowa Falls ethanol producer Hawkeye Holdings in May 2006, filed registration papers with the Securities & Exchange Commission (SEC) for Hawkeye to go public. The buyout transaction was followed immediately by an initial public offering (IPO) which reportedly generated a profit of US$312 million on the PE firm's investment – without any 'nurturing' of the investee company. Moreover, the PE firm charged Hawkeye an advisory fee of US$20 million for negotiating the buyout, US$1 million management fee and other payments totalling around US$27 million – despite Hawkeye's modest earnings of US$1.5 million over the first semester of 2006 (see Thornton, 2006, in the periodical *Business Week*, which is a sister company of the SEC-accredited major credit rating agency Standard & Poor's).

The nurturing function is, in principle, at the very core of the PE business (this subject is developed further in Chapter 3). Nevertheless, some PE firms acquired companies with the intention of selling them immediately afterwards (see Thornton, 2006). Sufficiently long periods of entrepreneurial funding provide investee companies with time to commit talent and other resources to promising strategies.

Critics have attributed to a few PE top executives motives of being lured by propects of personal *power* and excessive *profits* – verging on covetousness or greed – often demonstrated in lavish ostentatious consumption. An environment of opacity or partial disclosure of material information, along with the absence of regulatory frameworks to protect stakeholders, can foster such questionable practices (see Exhibit 2.1).

Exhibit 2.1 Examples of queried practices in the PE business

1 Potential winners

PE firms

- Even if no profits are made, PE firms charge fees (notably management fees of up to 2 per cent on assets). The foregoing fee is in addition to a hefty 'carry' on the up-side of profitable individual investments (20 per cent or more of net wealth generated above a 'hurdle rate'), and regardless of losses incurred on other investments.
- PE firms could oblige investee companies to incur debt to pay out dividends to their PE funds (in which the PE firms are shareholders), although the investee companies could be encountering funding problems (a practice referred to as 'dividend recapitalization').
- PE firms' management (the general partners) take their 20 per cent 'carry' share upfront even before their investors (the limited partners) break even with their 'hurdle rate'.

Banks

- PE firms' investment banks charge large fees for brokering and advising on mergers and acquisitions (M&A), underwriting debt, selling through IPO (initial public offering) a privately-held company, and other functions.

2 Potential losers

Shareholders of publicly-traded acquisitions

- Sizeable PE firms could acquire publicly-traded companies at prices below 'fair value', notably if they club together in an 'investment syndicate' and if they can entice the top management of the targeted company to acquiesce to such prices – possibly in return for keeping this management at the helm of the acquired company, luring them with large compensation packages and other benefits such as 'carry'.

- Erstwhile shareholders of an acquired company could feel short-changed (that is, paid below the 'fair price') if the PE firm sells the freshly acquired company at a significantly higher price, soon after its acquisition, without any value creation or 'nurturing' by the PE firm.

Investors

- A PE fund's investors (the limited partner) cannot monitor the fund's management (the general partner).

Employees of portfolio companies

- Risks of possible job losses when PE firms are more focused on improving the financial results of their acquired companies over the short term, in order to re-sell them soon after acquisition; significant long-term investment for the development/commercialization of new products or technologies are forsaken.

Customers, suppliers and creditors

- Customers, suppliers and subcontractors are vulnerable to possible frequent changes in the top management of PE investee companies they deal with, should these companies pass from one PE firm's ownership to another.
- Loading investee companies with excessive new debt can provoke their financial distress and hurt their creditors, as interest rates rise or profits plummet.

Local/national communities

- PE firms' unwarranted downsizing or delocalization of investee companies' activities would have an adverse impact on the prosperity of local businesses and the tax revenues of the authorities.

Sources: Cases illustrating the above-mentioned risks have been reported by regulatory agencies and the media. See, for example, Financial Services Authority, 2006. Among media sources, see Weinberg and Vardi, 2006; Thornton, 2006; and Krantz, 2006.

As entrepreneurial financiers concerned with business development, PE firms can exercise a *propulsive* role on economic growth if they actively support over the medium/long term investee companies. Alternatively, PE firms may have a *dampening* impact on economic growth if their objective is quick money either (a) by *re-selling* companies (acquired at low prices) soon after they control them and without adding real value; or (b) by *dismantling* businesses that would otherwise be prosperous given appropriate nurturing by competent management over a few years. PE management's nurturing of acquisitions can be both beneficial to the acquired companies and profitable to PE investors and other stakeholders (see Cao and Lerner, 2006; also *The Economist*, 2006a).

References

Blackstone Group, The (2003) Blackstone Announces Intention to Launch Friendly Takeover Offer for Celanese AG, 16 December.

Bloomberg Markets (2007) 'Pamela Daley Leads General Electric's $115 billion M&A Drive', *Bloomberg Markets*, May, pp. 30–42.

British Venture Capital Association (2006), *Private Equity – a UK Success Story* (London: IE Consulting), February.

Bygrave, William D. and Hunt, Stephen A. (2005) *GEM 2004 Financing Report* (London: Global Entrepreneurship Monitor), 31 May, p. 11.

Cao, Jerry (Boston College) and Lerner, Josh (Harvard Business School) (2006) *The Performance of Reverse Leveraged Buyouts*, Research paper, 22 May.

Economist, The (2004) 'The New Kings of Capitalism – A Survey of Private Equity', 27 November, p. 9.

Economist, The (2005a) 'German Capitalism – Locus, Pocus', 5 May.

Economist, The (2005b) 'Private Equity in Germany – Anglo-Saxon Attitudes', 17 December, p. 73.

Economist, The (2006) 'Alternative Investments – Doing Well by Doing Good', 30 September, p. 88.

Economist, The (2007) 'Investing in Distress – The Vultures Take Wing', 31 March, pp. 77–80.

Economist, The (2007c) 'Sovereign-wealth Funds', 26 May, pp. 79–80.

European Commission (2003) *SMEs and Access to Finance* (Brussels: European Commission).

Farrell, Diana and Lund, Susan (2008) 'The World's New Financial Power Brokers', *The McKinsey Quarterly*, no. 1, pp. 83–97.

Financial Services Authority (2006) *Private Equity: A Discussion of Risk and Regulatory Engagement* (London: FSA), November.

Financial Times (2006) 'FT Fund Management', 27 February, pp. 2–3.

Financial Times (2008) 'Interview with Philip Yea, CEO of 3i', 25 March, p. 15.

Hsu, David H. and Kenney, Martin (2004) *Organizing Venture Capital: The Rise and Demise of American Research & Development Corporation, 1946–1973*, Working paper 163, The Wharton School and University of California, Davis, December.

IFSL Research (2008a) *Sovereign Wealth Funds 2008* (International Financial Services London), April.

IFSL Research (2008b) *Private Equity 2008* (International Financial Services, London).

IMF (2008) *Sovereign Wealth Funds – A Work Agenda*, 29 February.

International Trade Union Confederation (2007) *Labour and the Shifting Power Equation,* Statement at the World Economic Forum Annual Meeting, Davos, Switzerland, 24–28 January.

Kern, Steffen (2007) *Sovereign Wealth Funds – State Investments on the Rise*, Frankfurt-am-Main: Deutsch Bank Research, 10 September.

Krantz, Matt (2006) 'Private Equity Firms Spin-off Cash', *USA Today,* 17 March.

Lai, Richard (2005) 'Explaining the Rise of Funds of Funds', Working paper, *Harvard Business School,* May.

Lambert, Richard, Director General, Confederation of British Industry (2007) Speech, 14 February.

Mason, Colin M. (2006) 'Informal Sources of Venture Finance', in Simon Parker (ed.), *The Life Cycle of Entrepreneurial Ventures: Vol. 3, International Handbook on Entrepreneurship* (Dordrecht: Kluwer Academic Publishers).

Mikdashi, Zuhayr (1998) *Les banques à l'ère de la mondialisation* (Banks in the Era of Globalization) (Paris: Economica) – in French.

Service Employees International Union (2008) 'Thousands Protest Tax Loopholes That Benefit Wealthy Buyout CEOs', Press release, 17 July.

Sovran, Joe (2006) 'Private Equity Funds of Funds', *Capvent AG.*

Tassell, Tony and Chung, Joanna (2007) 'How Sovereign Wealth Funds Are Muscling in on Global Markets', *Financial Times,* 24 May; available at: FT.com.

Thornton, Emily (2006) 'Gluttons at The Gate – Private Equity Are Using Slick New Tricks to Gorge on Corporate Assets: A Story of Excess', *Business Week,* 30 October.

Townley, Danforth (2006) 'Issues Facing Hedge Funds as They Adopt New Investment Strategies', *CapitalEyes,* Bank of America, September/October, pp. 2–4.

UNI Global Union (2007) *Private Equity – Looking for a Fairer Sharing of Risk and Reward*, Nyon, Switzerland.

Weinberg, Neil and Vardi, Nathan (2006) 'Private Inequity', *Forbes Magazine,* 13 March.

3
PE Leaders' Strategies

Private equity (PE) firms generally define their investment strategies in a 'private placement memorandum' addressed to potential investors. The memorandum presents various features: size of the fund, types of proposed investments, deal flow, fees, life cycle of the investment portfolio, expected return(s), the average debt/equity leverage in targeted acquisitions, and other key characteristics. Some PE funds may seek to own controlling interests in companies, while others opt for spreading risks through minority stakes in a variety of unrelated industries. A PE firm may solicit, to begin with, potential investors sharing similar objectives from among its traditional core clients. The circle could be enlarged to encompass other potential investors, should sums required prove difficult to mobilize within the core group.

The PE process and savvy decisions

In principle, PE funds seek to nurture, reorientate, redress, restructure or support the maturing process of their investee companies – with the ultimate goal of increasing their value appreciably by the end of a pre-set time horizon. In the nurturing process, for example, an 'add-on' (or 'buy and build') strategy is often used, which consists of augmenting the size of the investee company with additional acquisitions that fit in via complementarities (vertical or horizontal integration) or synergies (operational and financial) benefiting the combined entity. Such a strategy's success is measured by reference to its contribution to net gains before the pre-decided date of expiration of the fund's life (a ten- to twelve-year time horizon extending from *origination,* when investors agree to commit their capital, until the agreed date for *exiting* investments). Capital will then be returned to investors along with realized gains, as mandated in the relevant investment memorandum.

Exhibit 3.1 presents a *stylized* PE fund's cycle with key phases and tasks to be assumed by the concerned PE management. These tasks can be grouped in seven major phases as follows:

(a) constituting the PE management team and defining its strategy;
(b) fund raising: firm commitments by investors;
(c) search for, evaluation, selection, negotiation, due diligence, and ultimately investment (equity and debt) in promising targeted companies;
(d) nurturing investee companies through full co-operation with their management (assisting in streamlining/restructuring and development/expansion strategies);
(e) exiting investments opportunely through optimal routes when (it is hoped) significant gains are realizable; and
(f) distribution of the PE portfolio 'exit proceeds'.

PE firms may call as they see fit on the services of investment bankers, consulting houses, auditing groups, legal offices and other

Exhibit 3.1 A sequence of phases in the PE process

A. Sponsors agree on strategy, management team and setting up the PE Fund

B. Raising capital

- Private placement memorandum.
- Obtaining investors' financial commitments.
- Mobilization of funds.

C. Acquiring companies

- Sourcing with access to a wide deal flow (M&A advisers, financial intermediaries, legal/audit firms, entrepreneurs' associations, industry groups, PE associations and so on).
- Screen, analyse, evaluate and select potential acquisitions whose attractiveness is judged by macro and micro criteria,

using different methodologies and scenarios in reaching valuations (teamwork).

- Seller and buyer have a mutual interest in reaching a deal: they exchange information and negotiate.
- Due diligence (legal; accounting – financial; fiscal; customers – suppliers; waste management; and other issues).
- Secure debt financing.
- Conclude the deal transaction.

D. Creating net value

- Attractive acquisitions (timed when prices are moderate) with prospects for eventual exit options.
- Capital structuring of investee companies (debt – equity).
- Fiscal optimization.
- Financial reporting and discipline.
- Strategic leadership and managerial – technical support.
- Nurturing internally or by add-on.
- Oversight of portfolio companies.
- Risk management of the portfolio (including diversification of investments).
- Efficient, transparent, and speedy communication between the PE firm and the investee companies
- Hands-on management of distressed/ailing companies.

E. Evaluation of exits: timing and routes

- Timely exits of portfolio companies (when sale prices are deemed attractive) and before the end of the mandatory life span of the fund.
- Exit venues: sale of portfolio companies to other funds, IPOs, MBO, MBI, M&A sales to industrial/trade groups (see Chapter 4).

F. Distribution of the harvest's proceeds

- On the sale of investments and before the termination date of the PE partnership (as agreed in the 'private placement memorandum' – PPM), investors receive payment in cash or in shares.
- PE management cashes in its 'carry'.

G. Management of other funds

- The PE firm launches new funds.
- Appeal to existing and/or new categories of investors.

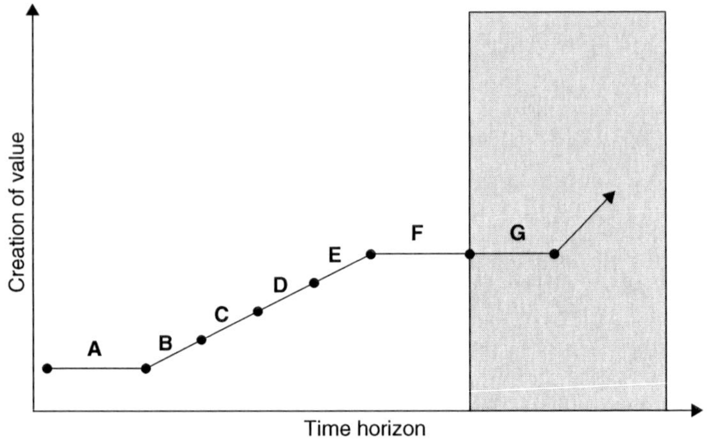

establishments when there is no suitable expertise available in-house. Naturally, executives of PE firms have to ascertain that deals proposed by investment bankers, and services provided by various other parties, are in their best interest. Investment bankers are important participants in PE deals, and their services cover mergers and acquisitions (M&A), underwriting, structuring the capital of client firms, initial public offerings (IPOs), and other services. Their performance rests on bringing efficiently to fruition the sale/purchase transactions, guided by the objective of value creation for the parties they are serving. To achieve this objective, an investment banking team should have in-depth knowledge of: the business sectors concerned, business leaders'/senior executives' characters, past and current business deals, and other matters that could help in identifying synergies (for example, the sale of a business to an industrial group) and/or other benefits.

For the mandate of selling a business, an investment bank (with an exclusivity right over an agreed period of some twelve months or more) charges its client enterprise a flat fee at the beginning of the mandate. The success fee is generally based on the equity of the business for sale, often starting with a minimum of 2 per cent and rising with increments of values obtained above a given threshold, usually up to 7 per cent, in order to induce the investment banker to obtain the highest possible value for the seller (see also chapter 4).

To generate comparatively high returns, the challenge for PE managers is to acquire promising companies at bargain prices very early in the upward phase of the business cycle. This would ideally be ahead of likely economic growth in the targeted sector, and before investors' euphoria bids up the value of targeted companies. Such an attractive acquisition moment could well be when markets overreact by undervaluing certain industries – for example, just after a financial crash or at the bottom of a trough in a business cycle. Anticipating the behaviour of investors and business cycles falls often in the realm of conjecture.

An owner's decision to sell his business must weigh personal considerations and propitious timing (see, for example, Allison, 2006). The terms and timing of decisions could call for bold and speedy action, relying significantly on gut feeling in the absence of perfect information and/or ample time to analyse data. Morever, decision-makers need to avoid being 'snowed under' by too much data, which cannot be properly ascertained, measured, interpreted or understood (see, for example, Gigerenzer and Selten, 2002; and Gigerenzer, 2006). The iconic investor Warren Buffett, CEO of Berkshire Hathaway, informed an audience of MBA students at IMD (Swiss business school in Lausanne) – that, for his first major non-US acquisition, a one-page letter was sufficient: he said the seller gave him 'basic facts and told me something about the person who ran [the company]'. *Intuition* underpinned by *experience* can thus prove of superior value to Buffett and other investors in comparison to complex *technical analyses* (see Karaian, 2008).

In the remaining sections of this chapter, the following issues are examined: the desirability of having a minority versus a majority interest in a target company; club deals; managing acquired companies; the negotiation process; and the optimization of capital structure and tax architecture of investee companies.

'Controlling' versus 'minority' interests

PE firms' approaches to acquisition are influenced by the targeted companies circumstances and prevailing business conditions. Three major investment options are usually examined: a total acquisition; a majority stake in the equity of the investee company; and a minority stake.

With a controlling interest of equity or voting rights of a target company, a PE firm can take an active role in setting the strategy of the acquired company. By nominating to the board of directors of the acquired company talented, experienced, and inquisitive persons, and by retaining or recruiting competent top managers, the PE firm can add value to the investee company. 'Majority' ownership enables PE executives to require full transparent reporting from acquired companies. The problem of opacity does not exist when the investing group is in a majority position – and accordingly able to demand from the investee company full compliance with the set strategy, and observance of cost controls and risk management directives.

A PE fund with limited financial resources, by following a strategy of acquiring the whole equity stake (or a controlling interest) in a few companies, could thus encounter the drawback of concentrating risks in a few enterprises. This would deny the PE fund's management the advantage of diversification through a multitude of minority interests – by spreading its financial resources and its risks/rewards widely over a larger number of enterprises (diversified by industry, size, country, year of investment, and other criteria).

Another related potential disadvantage of majority ownership by a PE firm is that of a possible liability *vis-à-vis* the acquired company, should the latter encounter unexpected difficulties. In that eventuality, the PE managers of the majority-owned company would have to take responsibility for their failure to steer the company towards profitability. Unless the PE firm revitalizes the distressed investee company with appropriate managerial talents and financial resources and turns it around, the company could become a total loss – to be disposed of to receivership or be dismantled with its assets (often sold at sacrificed prices).

For a safe strategy of diversification, several PE firms put a ceiling on each investment (for example, 10 per cent of their fund's resources) in order to spread their portfolio's risks. They will also seek to acquire companies from economic sectors that are not closely correlated with respect to their business cycles.

The drawback of acquiring minority interests in investee companies is that the PE fund's management would be placed in a passive situation. Indeed, if conditions go awry, the fund could be faced with a decline in the value of its minority-owned portfolio companies, with limited (or no) influence to redress the problem.

Minority interests in investee companies are mandatory for 'small business investment companies' (SBICs), as enacted by the US Congress in 1958. SBICs provide venture financing and management assistance to small companies in start-up and growth situations (whose net worth is less than $18 million, and net annual income less than $6 million). SBICs are closed-end investment companies, licensed and regulated by the US federal Small Business Administration (SBA). SBA's licensing requires (a) a minimum regulatory capital of $5 million supplied by private investors, and (b) a competent management under the purview of a board largely composed of qualified independent directors. SBA provides SBICs long-term funding (obtained through the sale of 10-year US Treasury bonds which carry an interest significantly below private funding). A ceiling of 20 per cent of the SBICs' regulatory capital is imposed on any investment in a single firm – for reasons of diversification. SBICs may control small businesses for up to seven years; the latter period is subject to extension with SBA approval. Small investors in the SBICs' publicly traded stocks have thus the opportunity of investing in the PE small-business class of assets.

To make diversification through minority interests productive, the PE fund concerned must make sure that it does not need to flex its muscles *vis-à-vis* the investee companies' management. The latter's quality – as judged by competence, honesty and motivation – and interests are deemed in line with those of PE investors. A prior agreement among major PE co-investors for the oversight of an investee company, and for reaching and implementing strategic decisions – such as exit strategies – may avert potential conflicts and protect the interests of core stakeholders.

An investor's majority stake in a company (more than 50 per cent of equity and/or voting rights) generally commands a premium value in the market, in comparison with a minority interest. Such a premium for a majority stake derives from a PE firm's capacity to exercise full authority over the investee company – notably with respect to:

(i) defining the company's business strategies of future development (whether from within the firm or through acquisitions that create appreciable complementarities or synergies);
(ii) monitoring and overseeing management's performance;

(iii) the timely provision of expertise and other resources – as and when warranted – to improve the investee company's opportunities and/or to contain its risks; and
(iv) deciding the sale the acquired company at the most opportune time and best possible price.

A PE firm that agrees to buy the majority of a company can require a drag-along clause. Such a clause authorizes the majority owner to force minority shareholders to participate in the eventual sale of the company on the same terms, and assures the prospective buyer that s/he will gain full control of the company. The clause normally enables the majority shareholder to obtain a better price from the acquirer than would be the case in the absence of such a provision.

Nevertheless, and notwithstanding the fine quality of management and its solid achievements at the time of acquisition, a PE firm with a controlling interest in an investee company is well advised to install an early warning system to detect failures and act without delay. Indeed, should management's quality deteriorate in later years, the PE firm that controls an enterprise can make timely interventions, as warranted.

Club deals

Large sums of money flowing into the PE sector have favoured the trend of targeting larger companies. Historically, the largest acquisition was that of RJR Nabisco (the US food and tobacco giant), completed in April 1989 by the PE firm Kohlberg Kravis Roberts (KKR) for US$31 billion (including debt). The transaction turned out to be an innovative approach concerning the structuring of the acquisition of a large company. In relation to return, however, it turned out to be a financial flop, with an internal rate of return of less than 1 per cent. The primary source of difficulty was that the operation was not conjugated with decisive improvements in the management of the acquired group. This episode has helped KKR to sharpen its strategy in later deals, thus bringing higher returns to its investors, partners and executives. Managers of investee companies appointed by KKR have reportedly become animated in their value creation goal by two basic concerns: *fear* of losing their own money which they have to invest in the acquired company, and the *incentive* of producing the highest possible financial returns (in which they share) within a limited time horizon before exiting the investee company (see Teitelbaum, 2007).

A couple of decades later (February 2007) KKR co-led with Texas Pacific Group (TPG) another mega-bid for the Texan energy firm TXU Energy, estimated at US$45 billion (including syndicated debt) – all figures in current dollars. Equity investments in the TXU Energy acquisition are US$2.5 billion for both KKR and TPG, Goldman Sachs US$1.5 billion and Lehman Brothers US$1 billion (*Financial Times,* 26 February 2007). This was followed by the acquisition of the Canadian telecom group BCE (Bell Canada Enterprises) in July 2007 for US$48.5 billion (including US$15.9 billion debt) by a consortium of investors comprising Ontario Teachers, Providence Equity Partners Inc., and Madison Dearborn LLC (www.bce.ca).

For large buyouts, PE firms may find it is in their interest to club together through a syndicate of investors and a joint shareholders' pact in which they agree on key issues. The latter include agreeing on: the lead negotiator; setting an acceptable acquisition price range; funding strategy (core equity, senior debts, mezzanine and other subordinated debts, bridge or medium-term financing, and other related subjects); the choice of a management team capable of implementing the club's defined business strategies; industry expertise to be offered along with oversight of the acquired company's management; eventual add-on acquisitions or spin-offs; and exit strategies in terms of timing, methods of sale and acceptable sale prices.

The approach of clubbing is generally *ad hoc,* with no obligation for participants to conduct future club deals. These deals allow partnering PE firms to (a) jointly mobilize larger resources to acquire bigger companies; (b) eliminate rivalry and price competition among club members who act as a single consortium, thereby avoiding the costly auctioning process leading to the bidding-up of the prices of targeted acquisitions and over-valuation; (c) share their particular insights, diverse experiences of particular sectors or markets, variety of perspectives, and/or solutions in relation to complex and sizeable targeted businesses; and (d) spread costs and risks among club members.

Co-investment funds that participate in club deals are induced by (a) their trust for the broad *industry expertise* of the lead PE firm in originating the business opportunity; (b) significant *synergies* with the club leader; and (c) the *lower fees* they would have to pay for the deal, compared to regular PE investors. Should co-investor funds be solicited on an *ad hoc* basis, there is always the risk of possible delays in the decision-making process, because of protracted negotiations. There can also be a possible risk for a co-investor with respect to 'lack of adequate diversification' – should that co-investor not be involved systematically in all co-investments with the lead PE fund. One could imagine that co-investors – notably the high net worth persons and the institutional ones – have their own diversification strategies (see Bank of America, 2005; and *The Economist,* 2006).

To summarize, chief challenges or issues in club deals – compared with a go-it-alone approach by a PE fund – cover the following:

(i) delays in the decision-making process;
(ii) a concern for possible anti-trust probes with a risk of charges regarding collusion to thwart competition and keep acquisition prices artificially low;
(iii) the club's initiator and leader may to obliged to forgo or reduce the 'carry' fee (averaging about 20 per cent of the 'capital gain' above an agreed hurdle rate) from invited co-investors;
(iv) the problematic availability of bank funding at reasonable terms for mega-deals;
(v) the reticence of targeted investee companies *vis-à-vis* clubs of PE firms;
(vi) possible difficulties among club participants in agreeing on the strategies of running the investee companies; and/or
(vii) the favourable publicity and prestige that would accrue to the PE firm that 'goes it alone' as the sole master of a mega-deal (see Kelly and Evans, 2007).

Managing acquired companies

The most important asset of an enterprise is generally its human capital, to be distinguished from material capital (that is, financial resources, equipment, real estate, raw materials and other physical assets). For the 1992 Nobel Prize laureate in economics, Gary S. Becker, 'economists regard expenditures on education, training, medical care, and so on as investments in *human* capital. They are called human capital because people cannot be separated from their knowledge, skills, health, or values in the way they can be separated from their financial and physical assets' (Gary S. Becker, 'Human Capital', *The Concise Encyclopedia of Economics*). It is thus crucial for the acquirer of an enterprise to retain managers and employees who create value (especially those who cannot readily be replaced). The PE firm therefore needs to win their confidence and enlist their support. In its acquisition policy, the PE firm can choose between two main approaches – with the possibility of several intermediate variants. The decision depends on the perceived expected advantages, in the light of circumstances obtaining at the time of transaction. The two major alternatives, illustrated below by reference to FBs/SMEs, are:

(i) To maintain the previous owner-manager over an agreed time horizon; s/he could be offered a managerial, consulting or coaching role – possibly buttressed by keeping an equity interest in the investee company; and
(ii) To sever all links and influences of the previous owner or top manager of the acquired company, immediately upon signature of the acquisition transaction, while in parallel promoting from within or parachuting from outside a new CEO.

Continuity of management

Retaining the incumbent entrepreneur-owner/manager (along with his/her key associates) at the helm of the acquired enterprise is advisable, especially if s/he has company-specific human capital. Such continuity, at least for an interim period, will allow the acquirer to benefit from his/her experience and managerial talent. The solicited party needs naturally to have the drive to continue in his/her responsibilities subject to an attractive compensation package and assuming s/he enjoys good health to enable him/her to carry on leading the business.

The PE negotiator would hope to succeed in convincing the abovementioned owner-manager to accept a 'not-too-inflated' price for relinquishing control of his/her enterprise, while remaining at the helm of the business for an agreed time. The owner – who has been proved to be honest in presenting the strengths and weaknesses of his/her company during the negotiations – can thus continue to increase the wealth of the company in which s/he remains a significant shareholder. His/her interests will thus be closely aligned to those of investors (sharing in both risks and rewards).

The retention of the selling owner-manager mentioned above as CEO (assuming s/he maintains a significant stake in the equity of the investee company) will enable the acquirers to (a) make good use of his/her valuable insights, creativity, business know-how and leadership; (b) preserve the knowledge and experience of loyal personnel attached to the CEO; (c) foster the web of existing human and business relations among various parties linked to the acquired enterprise; and (d) groom upcoming management. The advantages of the retention of the selling owner for a transitory period applies clearly to cross-border acquisitions, when those responsible for the PE fund do not have an in-depth knowledge of local markets and of the socio-economic environment.

The direct involvement of the founder or owner-manager of an enterprise has a positive effect on the firm's performance, according to an empirical investigation (see Villalonga and Amit, 2004). The owner-manager has to be convinced of the benefits he can obtain from partnering (as a minority shareholder) with the investing PE fund. S/he should be convinced of: the acquirer's business plan and strategy, the financial structure (including the reasonableness of the level and terms of financial leverage) of the deal, and other key matters.

The selling owner-manager's network of relationships represents an intangible economic asset of tremendous value for the acquired business. This asset can serve the upcoming management considerably – in so far as it provides them with the opportunity of learning from the experiences of the veteran CEO and from his/her seasoned judgement, in order to avoid pitfalls, rationalize operations and make productive use of potential opportunities. 'Internal coaching' by the erstwhile owner-manager would generally prove to be superior to external coaching of a new top management (see *The Economist*, 2003). In agreement with the acquirers, the selling owner can programme, as needed, his/her exit from any equity stake that s/he might have retained – at the optimal time and on agreeable terms for both parties – when a new team has been properly groomed to take over the responsibilities of top management.

Installing a new management

Installing a new management in a newly acquired company is warranted when the erstwhile owners–managers have indicated their wish to retire. With a 'clean' slate of authority and responsibility, a newly installed management will avoid possible drawbacks of retaining the selling owner. Among these drawbacks, one could notably mention:

(a) a duality in the loyalty of certain members of the personnel *vis-à-vis* previous top managers (the old guard) versus the new ones;
(b) lingering nepotism or cronyism that might have a negative effect on professionalism;
(c) possible delays in the eventual overhaul of strategy and/or in the streamlining of the company's activities; or
(d) jealousy or a clash in styles of management between the *incumbent* and *incoming* managers.

Nevertheless, the acquirer would normally weigh the possible loss of know-how and details of business relationships accumulated by the previous owner–manager should the latter's departure be abrupt. An adequate transition period is needed for the smooth and effective transfer of that know-how to the new management. This transition could take less time if management is recruited from within, as opposed to outside management. The transition involves many functions to be carried out by the departing owner–manager: introducing the new CEO to employees, customers, suppliers, bankers and so on; familiarizing him or her with the strategies and practices of the business; apprising him/her of the company's manufacturing or technical secrets; and other matters relating to competition, product development, human resources, customers and partners. Moreover, it is crucial for the new management to rapidly win the confidence and commitment of the personnel. The erstwhile CEO could be induced to remain for a short period, possibly with the status of external consultant – subject to the absence of conflicts of interest. S/he could perhaps even finish selected business projects or tasks (for example, relating to clients, suppliers, subcontractors or others).

Empirical evidence regarding the relative merits of recruiting CEOs for newly acquired enterprises from within (as opposed to external recruitment) are inconclusive. Some research studies suggest that the acquisition of a firm by top management from within the acquired business assuming the existence of qualified talents (that is, management buy-out – MBO) produce superior performances compared to calling on *external* managers (that is, management buy-in – MBI) for such an acquisition. The differences in performance may well generally result from the superior company-specific knowledge and experience of top management recruited from within the firm, compared to managers brought in from outside the investee firms. Higher performance of the MBO strategy are supported by systematic evidence from 12,267 UK buyouts transacted over the period 1985–2005 (see Wright *et al.*, 2007).

Other empirical investigations, however, find that 'for companies involved in private equity transactions, including both buy-out (LBO) and venture capital (VC) ... outside CEO candidates are more highly rated than incumbents' (Kaplan *et al.*, 2007). External CEOs could bring valuable experiences and new productive perspectives. In a survey of French companies undertaken in 2005, some two-thirds of acquirers of enterprises have favoured using, over a transitional period, the expertise of the erstwhile owner–manager (see *L'Usine Nouvelle,* 2007). In order to align the interests of newly-installed management with those of the PE firm, the new managers need to be motivated by incentives (competitive salaries and ownership stakes). Such incentives will then ensure that management will be driven to maximize value creation for the benefit of all owners and other stakeholders (see Chapter 5). This should not preclude the PE executives concerned from exercising (at the board of directors' level of investee companies) vigilant oversight and providing strategic insights within their areas of expertise. For such involvement, PE executives need to have an in-depth knowledge of targeted companies.

Negotiation or auction: technical and psychological skills

PE managers typically search for a large number of investment opportunities, which they screen with a view to selecting those that best meet their fund's criteria. For a typical buyout PE fund specializing in growth or mature companies, the targeted enterprise is generally acquired with some 50 to 60 per cent debt leverage, the financial charges of which (repayment of principal and payment of interest and commissions) should not penalize the solvency and growth of the enterprise. Generally within an average five-year period, the PE fund expects to repay its debt and exit from the investment with a comfortable added value (see, for example, Andrea, 2006).

Several PE firms prefer the 'negotiated approach' in so far as this puts them in a better position to shape the deals, with a view to improving or protecting their returns on investment. 'Off-market' deals – in contrast to auctions – are generally less amenable to overbidding. Seldom do the successful sale of small firms go through the 'auction' process, however.

A PE transaction by negotiation between the PE firm and the investee company is the end result of a lengthy gradualist and cumulative process – with twists and turns – that culminates in a mutually satisfactory structuring of the terms of ownership transfer. In honing their strategies and practices, successful acquirers set a *studied* walk-away price at the outset to avoid the eventuality of being carried away by emotion and pay an *inflated price* under conditions of intense rival bidding to clinch a deal. Such a price can depress the PE fund's expected ultimate return for its investors, calculated at the winding-up of the fund.

The time spent on negotiation – much longer than that for auctions – allows the buyers to understand fully the motivations and aspirations of the company's owners who seek to sell their enterprises, and to become familiar with managers – notably those who might remain in the enterprise. Through the negotiation process, a PE fund can accommodate with greater flexibility any reasonable wishes of sellers, while avoiding rash decisions. Indeed, the PE negotiator should be cautious *vis-à-vis* an owner who is eager to sell his/her enterprise – in case there are hidden liabilities that have not been disclosed earlier by due diligence.

Exhibit 3.1, on page 80 above, presents a typical pattern of the main sequential stages (with possible time overlap of tasks among some of the stages) that lead to the conclusion of a PE transaction by negotiation. The PE 'deal-maker' is likely to consist of a team led by an experienced and knowledgeable executive, who establishes the strategy of acquisition/sale. His strategy is usually guided by the directives of the PE fund's investment committee, which vets investment opportunities using rigorous criteria and benchmarks. Larger investors could have an important role in the PE fund – for example, on the fund's advisory board or its investment committee.

The business plan of the targeted enterprise is a central piece in the PE negotiation–transaction process. It articulates over a medium-term horizon (usually five years ahead) key factors that would shape the investment's profitability. Realistic assumptions are used, based on the reliable consolidated reporting of the targeted enterprise along with due consideration of competitors' market position. Key factors of the business plan include, in particular, details on key prospective conditions such as sales and purchases (split into markets); accounts receivable and changes in their duration; prices/costs of products and inputs; profit margins; shareholders equity; projected investments; size of borrowing and debt charges; cash flows; salaries of managers and employees; employees' turnover; eventual losses; taxes; and other operational and financial data.

Among the commonly used financial measures of valuation of privately-held companies, one can mention the method that relies on *multiples* of certain industry averages: notably EBIT (earnings before interest and taxes), EBITDA (earnings before interest, taxes, depreciation and amortization), and P/E (price of traded shares over earnings) of *comparable* exchange-listed companies that are similar to the targeted privately-held company (with respect to product mix, risk conditions, and prospects of earnings and growth). Several other measures of valuation (such as the internal rate of return/discounted cash flow – IRR/DCF – methods) could be used for purposes of cross-checking before reaching a reasonable valuation estimate of an enterprise. All these measures have to be used justifiably and consistently throughout the life of the PE fund. Scenarios of possible and probable future performances have to allow for future contingencies.

Acquirers of a business need to adopt an inquisitive approach in their appraisal and not take figures at face value. This could be time-consuming (possibly extending over several months). Some length of time may be needed to unearth hitherto undetected problems such as excessive concentration or under-pricing of risks, irregular accounting, unresolved litigations, off-balance-sheet obligations (fiscal and others), personnel issues, environmental violations, intellectual property rights, information technology (IT) problems, opaque non-arm's-length transactions, among others.

Often sellers seek to prepare their companies for sale by cutting to an excessive extent current or capital expenditures to enhance profitability in the latest reported period. Such practices should not escape the attention of the inquisitive buyer. Buyers and sellers of PE stakes generally agree on price adjustment mechanisms, should there be significant divergences in the financial performance measures in the post-closing period (extending over one year, possibly more) by comparison with the latest period used as a basis for the negotiated price. Certain precautionary measures are resorted to, such as the postponement of the payment of a portion of the agreed price at acquisition, warranties, indemnities, and/or escrow deposits, in order to meet the above-mentioned contingencies of undetected liabilities or expenses. Often, the seller or the buyer may wish to have a 'clean' transaction without clauses for contingencies, in order to avoid being embroiled in future negotiations or litigations, and thus avoid being distracted by such eventual problems. Such a clean or up-front sale can be realized when both parties establish a trusting and transparent relationship. The ultimate conclusion of a transaction is likely to be made at the propitious time when the contracting parties' objective and subjective interests meet. Such a convergence would often call for trade-offs and compromises.

Beyond fending-off eventual risks pertaining to the acquired enterprise, buyers generally seek protection against 'material adverse change' resulting from calamities external to the firm – such as natural disasters or economic crises – that threaten the economic viability of the firm. Barring such dramatic eventualities, a PE firm could renege on its contractual obligation to consummate an acquisition transaction (for example, as a result of the difficulty of obtaining adequate financing). Should this happen, the PE firm concerned could be sued by the targeted company and could be obligated to pay a hefty 'break-up fee' commensurate to the imputed damage sustained by the to-be-acquired company (see Hahn, 2008).

The length of the negotiation period leading up to an acquisition would be influenced by several interwined factors, among which are: the nature of the business, market conditions, legal systems, and the local socio-cultural environment. The PE executive has to tread a fine line between (a) 'rushing' into a transaction, and thus missing important information on undisclosed critical matters that could have an adverse effect on the value of the acquisition; and (b) 'dragging out' negotiations, thereby risking losing the opportunity to clinch an attractive deal. The PE executive may choose to start by offering a 'low' price for the acquisition, should s/he imagine that the seller would feel psychologically 'better' when the final offer improves significantly on the initial price. Certain catalytic factors (for example, a positive 'personal chemistry' of empathy and mutual trust) can speed up the consummation of a deal.

In sum, factors which influence the time needed for an acquisition deal comprise:

(i) the collection and analysis of the requisite information by the prospective buyer;
(ii) the normal unfolding of the negotiation process, including the agreement over the acquisition price (or price range) subject to mutually acceptable covenants and conditions realized before the final transfer of ownership;
(iii) confirmation of the existing management or appointment of a revamped/reinvigorated management capable of mastering any future strategic challenges faced by the acquired business; and
(iv) the installation, for the benefit of the 'new owners', of an efficient reporting/monitoring/oversight system to protect their interests.

Given the traditional opacity of FBs, and more generally SMEs, the PE fund manager may have to resort to a detective-like collection and piecing together of reliable information, in order to obtain a reasonably objective and complete assessment of the target company. Owners and managers of SMEs are concerned that 'premature' disclosure of proprietary data, lest this be used by competitors to take advantage of insider information but with no genuine commitment to realize a deal. Furthermore, it is not uncommon that FBs in certain countries officially declare biased data (for example, only a proportion of their sales) for reasons of tax evasion (see *PME Magazine*, 2007). Prospective buyers of companies can possibly gain some useful insights from a variety of sources: bankers, credit registries, rating agencies, customers, suppliers, whistleblowers (if any), judiciary quarters, regulatory agencies, lawyers, circles of acquaintances, the media, governmental or parliamentary investigations, and others. The gathering of information can be costly and time-consuming. Nevertheless, knowledge is an economic asset, and its availability is an undeniable advantage to the PE fund. 'Word-of-mouth' information – generally obtained from various stakeholders – is bound to be valuable in so far as it complements scant data available to the public, and authenticates statements. The media and their investigative correspondents could be another source of insights. Troubled private firms faced with litigation (from different sources) could be obliged to disclose their problems in court, and court records accessible to the public could prove to be quite an important source of knowledge for potential investors.

Superior deal makers are considered to have special talents and skills (for example, courtesy, communication and persuasion) and are deeply sensitive to cultural values, business habits and social mores (in both local and foreign communities). An FB for sale could have among its owners other family members and friends. The PE fund's negotiator would then have to cater tactfully for the legitimate interests of various owners and other stakeholders, deftly using skills of enticement, thereby avoiding costly protracted negotiations, blockages or even lawsuits. It is not exceptional to find founders of family businesses mixing personal affairs (such as the use of cars, property or secretarial facilities) with strictly business activities. An FB with a transparent reporting system (for example, using international accounting norms in lieu of succinct information) commands a premium payable by potentially interested buyers. It provides these buyers with the confidence that the necessary knowledge is available.

A few FBs show significant divergences or intrigues – occasionally verging on visceral hatreds – among family owners (who could also be in the employ of the targeted firm), which cloud or distort their professional objectivity and hurt the prospects of the enterprise. In the event of the succession of the founding entrepreneur, an optimal approach would be to decouple 'ownership' from 'management' by entrusting management to highly competent professionals by means of enticing compensation packages linked directly to their performance. The foregoing arrangement should ensure that family members do not interfere unjustifiably in the running of the business.

Beyond obtaining the owners' agreement to the terms of a transaction, the PE fund's negotiator has to win the trust of other stakeholders (key segments of management and employees, creditors, major clients, suppliers, subcontractors and so on) in order to conclude a PE deal that protects the growth prospects of the investee company. An astute deal-maker can resort to the art and practice of *wooing* the management of the targeted company. This may be done through occasions of bonding – for example, during informal dining – to share information and views.

In any deal, a negotiator does not win on all points. Accordingly, with good judgement s/he prioritizes the most important issues. Depending on their respective hierarchies of values, a negotiating buyer could accept compromises and contractually concede to the counter-party certain demands. These demands might include the commitment to maintain over a given period of time certain activities to allay major concerns of key stakeholders (such as employees, customers or local authorities) in the targeted company.

The paths of specious proofs or arguments, brinkmanship and arrogance, and the deliberate hiding of critical information are strewn with pitfalls, and could prove counter-productive. Indeed, reputations for honesty, fair play and reliability are bound to be prized qualities by all parties concerned with finalizing business transactions.

It is not uncommon to find shrewd or clever sellers of enterprises playing off, openly or covertly, one potential buyer against another, in order to increase the price tag. In such circumstances, the buyer must exercise vigilance and guard against being manipulated or put on standby for an unduly protracted period. The buyer needs to avoid accepting 'stiff' prices for non-realistic reasons – while accommodating the non-costly hubris of the seller, for example maintaining the founder's name in the acquired company (see also Lewicki *et al.*, 2001).

In the final stage, the deal has to be drafted to reproduce the agreed decisions regarding the acquisition. The more details that are included, the better is the scope for avoiding possible misunderstanding and litigation in the future. Experienced lawyers are solicited to make sure that no loopholes remain, and that the provisions of the contract comply with the laws and regulations that apply in the jurisdictions concerned.

Capital and tax structures

PE firms seek naturally to maximize their returns, by reducing, *inter alia*, their financial costs. Two intertwined areas are crucial to that endeavour: structuring the capital of PE firms' portfolio companies, and choosing the legal domiciliation of entities holding the stakes of ownership in the said companies. Key aspects of these areas are examined below.

Structuring the capital of acquired companies

The architecture of a PE fund's financing an acquisition can prove crucial to investors' return. A PE fund can inject three categories of financial resources in the acquisition of an investee company: (a) equity, leveraged or supplemented by (b) 'near equity' (such as mezzanine or subordinated debt) and/or (c) other categories of medium/long-term and short-term debt. Banking and non-banking sources of debt finance to a company become more easily available at reasonable terms, if significantly underwritten by the PE fund's own capital stake in the said company.

Some PE funds resort to highly leveraged buyout (LBO) acquisitions since their borrowings provide a shield from corporate tax payments (knowing that debt charges are generally tax deductible before the calculation of corporate taxable income).The target companies' capital structures (that is, the composition of their debt–equity components) have to be studied carefully and properly calibrated in relation to the expected size and stability of net cash flows of each acquired company and the terms of third-party financing (interest charges, period, seniority, instalments, covenants, among others; see J. and K. Lewellen, 2005).

A pecking order is often resorted to in the structuring of capital for the acquisition of companies. This takes into consideration that higher risks (notably a higher degree of uncertainty with respect to the size and stability of expected cash flows) and more stringent conditions of borrowing call for the provision of a higher percentage of risk capital: starting with equity, followed by high-yield mezzanine and/or subordinated debt convertible into equity. Should a target company already be heavily indebted when judged by industry standards, it is risky for the acquirer to resort to sizeable LBO financing – other things remaining equal.

Traditional senior loans carry strict requirements – such as the obligation to repay the loans immediately should the borrower's profitability deteriorate (as defined by rigorous adherence to agreed 'financial ratio' standards) and/or the lender's right to increase interest rates. With large amounts of liquidity available in financial markets and intense competition among lenders (for example, during the period 2002–7; see also Chapter 1), 'covenant-lite' loans have become common. These loans, notably in the USA, are characterized by comparatively loose lending terms allowing borrowers to deviate from the conventional standards of required performance criteria – for example allowing them to pay off their outstanding financial charges by incurring additional debt (see Bank of England, 2007; also Thornton, 2007, and Kelly, 2007).

According to one banking source, 'Banks can earn considerably higher margins on loans to private equity firms than with traditional corporate lending. In addition to the upfront fee of around 2 per cent of the loan amount, a risk premium or margin of some 200 to 300 basis points is charged' (see Schaaf, 2005). Assuming easy market conditions for lending, the PE firm can create competition among its potential lending institutions to obtain comparatively attractive loan terms (interest, risk premiums, fee charges, and reimbursement schedules) – especially if the targeted acquisition has a comfortable predictable cash flow underpinned by the expansion of business turnover (see Lopez, 2008).

Fiscal competition

Firms in an open world economy tend to choose legal structures and domiciles that offer the least burdens (fiscal and social charges, regulatory and administrative requirements, and others) in order to maximize their returns. Chief among corporate costs, one could mention: tax charges; reporting and disclosure requirements; labour, social and environmental exigencies; accounting standards and methods (for example, with respect to flexibility of setting inter-affiliate transfer pricing, book versus market pricing of assets or liabilities, the expensing of certain expenditures); and others. Fiscal charges can be considered a driving force in the development of an economic activity, such as that of the private equity (PE) sector. Indeed, this has been the case in the United Kingdom with respect to the 'carry' received by the PE firm's partners (20 per cent of the profit above the hurdle rate). The 'carry' is eligible for a 'capital gain tax treatment. The capital gains tax (CGT) on business assets held for at least ten years was reduced in 1998 from 40 per cent to 10 per cent. In 2000, the minimum holding period for business assets was again reduced, to five years, and in 2002 reduced further to only two years (see House of Commons, 2007).

The foregoing CGT benefits favouring the PE sector have been considered a source of distortion in financial markets. It is argued that tax relief on the 'carry' is excessive, and provides an unfair competitive advantage by lowering the cost of capital for PE funds and lowering the taxation of PE firms' partners and their investors (see Tax Research LLP-UK, 2007).

To the extent that their portfolio companies operate across various markets, PE firms have some leeway in structuring their PE funds holding groups and in lodging them in countries that offer favourable tax and/or regulatory treatment. This involves, *inter alia*, ensuring optimal legal vehicles that are the least burdensome with respect to determining the *perimeter* of revenues or assets subject to taxation and the *rates* at which they are taxed – in order to maximize investors' benefits. Companies, if authorized, would shed one corporate structure in favour of another – to reduce their tax burdens or those of their investors (see, for example, *The Economist*, 2005a).

The return on an acquisition is bound to improve by making good use of tax-friendly jurisdictions. The latter are recognized as a result of a multitude of measures that culminate in lower tax burdens: for example, tax exemptions or allowances, low tax rates, protection against double taxation, generous tax deductions (for example, for *goodwill*), the expensing or the accelerated depreciation of capital expenditures, and allowing for losses abroad to be claimed at home. For the latter, a ruling by the European Union Court of Justice on 14 December 2005 allows cross-border tax relief on losses of business groups' subsidiaries abroad to be offset against profits made at home – so long as there was no prospect of future profits in the foreign country concerned (see *Financial Times*, 2005).

Governments may thus use various incentives to attract businesses and/or favour investors. These incentives could materialize by reducing the taxable income base and/or by reducing the tax rates applying to businesses or their employees. The chosen jurisdiction for domiciling a company, one should presume, needs to enjoy a sound reputation (on such matters as money laundering) in order to be acceptable to the international financial community. Tax competitiveness among various jurisdictions is well documented (see, for example, Mintz, 2007; available at: www.cdhowe.org). Companies operating in several countries may have the scope of setting transfer prices among affiliates – in the absence of market or arm's-length prices. The logic of optimizing fiscal burdens for a transnational corporation operating in such circumstances is to assign – to the extent that laws allow such practices – lower taxable profits to affiliates based in jurisdictions of higher taxation (and vice versa). Increasingly, fiscal authorities are wary of such corporate practices, and are able to counter them more-or-less successfully (see, for example, *The Economist*, 2005b).

Among the various fiscal incentives resorted to, one potent instrument is to charge retained earnings at a lower tax rate; by using internal cash for investments rather than paying it out as dividends to equity owners, the latter obtain in effect a deferral of personal taxes – other things remaining equal – thus making internal equity less costly than external equity, for tax reasons (see J. and K. Lewellen, 2005). In these circumstances, companies would prefer to finance their expansion through retained earnings rather than calling on *fresh* external equity.

Fiscal exemption of capital gains, for example, exists in Switzerland. In the USA, nearly all the PE firms (apart from a small handful) have adopted the limited partnership structure – mainly privately held partnerships, with a few publicly traded partnerships. Since the mid-1980s, US federal tax legislation has allowed PE partners (the GP) a favourable 15 per cent tax rate on their 'carry' (treated as a capital gain) earned from investments, instead of the 'ordinary income' tax rate of up to 35 per cent paid by corporate executives in high income brackets. The GP's 'carry' typically represents 20 per cent of the capital gains of the PE's investment portfolio above an agreed hurdle rate, realized at exit (see also Chapter 5). By comparison, the GP's management fee (on average 2 per cent of a fund's assets), is taxed as 'ordinary income'. The Private Equity Council, the Washington trade association comprising the largest US-based PE firms, has been lobbying Congress since 2007 not to increase capital gains tax (see: www.privateequitycouncil.org; also Fitzgerald and Salant, 2007).

In the United Kingdom, the 'carry' earned by PE firms' executives – also standing, as previously mentioned, at 20 per cent of investment gains above an agreed hurdle rate – has been treated as a 'capital gain' taxable at 10 per cent – if investments are held for more than two years, as mentioned above – compared to the top income tax rate of 40 per cent. Nicholas Ferguson, Chairman of SVG Capital (the biggest investor – €3.8 billion – in a large UK-based PE fund, Permira, of €14.8 billion) observed in 2007 that executives of PE firms were paying tax at a lower level than cleaners or other low-paid workers (interviewed by the *Financial Times*, 4 June 2007). Not only is that tax rate skewed in favour of PE executives compared to other taxpayers, it also tilts investments towards the 'short-term' for PE executives and their investors. Indeed, the latter are thus encouraged to dispose of acquired assets and companies by the end of the legally authorized minimum two-year period without nurturing them with long-term commitments (for example, through: investments in 'research and development', the internal expansion of activities, add-ons, or other strategies).

Members of the European Union (EU) continue to use tax competition to attract productive investments (see, for example, Quitzau, 2006). Moreover, the scope for tax avoidance (to be distinguished from tax evasion through unauthorized practices) exists within a single sovereign state. While federal taxes are uniform (for example, in the USA and Switzerland), corporate and/or personal fiscal charges vary considerably among the federated subnational jurisdictions. Thus some cantons within the Swiss federal state offer to negotiate significant tax reductions or exemptions for long or indeterminate periods for the benefit of resident enterprises or individuals (see details at: www.estv.ch).

The policy of reducing the tax base or rates – possibly leading to a situation of *tax haven* jurisdiction – aims to attract the domiciling and investments of foreign businesses and/or high-net-worth individuals whose spending is deemed to be beneficial to the domestic economy. Such a policy needs to be carefully calibrated in order to avoid undue erosion of the authorities' tax revenues that are needed for the provision of 'public goods' (such as security, justice, social safety nets, basic health, education and so on) incumbent on a modern state. Favouring the high income brackets of society could be resisted by other parties (guided by the principles of fairness and solidarity) in the state concerned. A reduction of taxation charges in a given jurisdiction would siphon off some business activities from other jurisdictions – unless the latter react to such encroachments by equivalent measures.

Federal states with subnational jurisdictions often encounter difficulties in harmonizing their tax and legal regimes. 'Excessive fiscal competition threatens to kill [*sic*] federalism' – a local Minister of Finance for the Swiss canton of Vaud warned (see Broulis, 2006). Thus the canton of Obwalden offers, since 2006, the lowest corporate tax rate for domiciled companies (13.1 per cent) – undercutting the canton of Schwyz (15.6 per cent) and Zug (16.4 per cent) – traditionally the lowest tax cantons. The Swiss Federal Finance Minister, Hans-Rudolf Merz, has publicly welcomed increased tax rivalry among the country's twenty-six cantons with respect to companies or individuals. His argument is that such tax competition protects the citizen from the 'excessive tax appetite' of governments and promotes budgetary discipline (see *PME Magazine,* 2006). The European Union (EU) Commission deems the Swiss cantons' tax-break practices to be 'unfair competition', akin to state aid, favouring 'tax evasion' from the EU to Switzerland. Yet the Commission has tolerated the Irish Republic's cut in the corporate tax rate from 40 per cent in 1993 to 12.5 per cent since 2006 – far below the EU's 25 per cent average (OECD statistics; see also Zipfel, 2007; and www.idaireland.com).

Taxation systems applying to economic units are far from uniform, whether within or between countries. Tax differentiation among economic sectors or social strata can be justified if based on such criteria as: fairness; growth, the boosting of innovation, job creation, exports, and GNP; or support to disfavoured regions and people.

References

Allison, Kevin (2006) 'The Search for an Opportune Moment', *Financial Times,* 21 December, p. 8.

Andrea, Sylvie (2006) 'Bien choisir son actionnaire financier' (Choosing well one's financial shareholder), *L'Usine Nouvelle,* Paris, 6 July, pp. 68–70.

Bank of America (2005) 'The Pros and Cons of Private Equity "Club" Deals', *CapitalEyes*, Bank of America, September.

Bank of England (2007) 'Recent Developments in Loan Covenants', *Quarterly Bulletin 2007 Q2,* p. 195.

Broulis, Pascal (2006) 'Excessive Fiscal Competition Threatens to Kill Federalism', *Le Temps*, Geneva, 21 January, p. 14.

Economist, The (2003) 'Executive Coaching – Corporate Therapy', 15 November, p. 65.

Economist, The (2005a) 'Canada's Income Trusts', 24 September, p. 93.

Economist, The (2005b) 'Discord over Harmony', *The Economist,* 12 November, p. 94.

Economist, The (2006) 'Private Equity – Club Class', 30 September, pp. 86–8.

Financial Times (2005) 'Pyrrhic Victory for High Tax Regimes', 14 December, p. 14.

Fitzgerald, Alison and Salant, Jonathan D. (2007) 'Democrats Cool on Measures to Boost Taxes – Buyout Firms' Muscle', *Bloomberg Markets*, September, p. 16.

Gigerenzer, Gerd (2006) 'Bounded and Rational', in R. J. Stainton (ed.), *Contemporary Debates in Cognitive Science* (Oxford: Blackwell), pp. 115–33.

Gigerenzer, Gerd and Selten, Reinhard (2002) *Bounded Rationality – The Adaptive Toolbox* (Cambridge, Mass.: MIT Press), August.

Hahn, Avital Louria (2008) 'Starting Over – In the Wake of a Broken Deal, How Do Companies Move On?', *CFO Europe,* April, pp. 51–2.

House of Commons (2007) *Private Equity, Tenth Report of Session 2006–07* (London: The Stationery Office Limited), 30 July, p. 36.

Kaplan, Steven N., Klebanov, Mark M. and Sorensen, Morten (2007) 'Which CEO Characteristics and Abilities Matter?', Working paper, University of Chicago Graduate School of Business, June.

Karaian, Jason (2008) 'Management – From Omaha to the Alps', *CFO Europe Magazine*, July/August, p. 14.

Kelly, Jason (2007) 'The Backlash Against Buyouts', *Bloomberg Markets*, November, pp. 53–60.

Kelly, Jason and Evans, Edward (2007) 'Flying Solo', *Bloomberg Markets*, July, pp. 16–17.

Lewellen, Jonathan and Lewellen, Katharina (2005) 'Capital Structure Choices of Firms', Working paper, *Sloan School of Management–MIT*, February.

Lewicki, R. J., Saunders, D. M. and Minton, J. W. (2001) *Essentials of Negotiation* (Boston, Mass.: McGraw-Hill).

Lopez, Jose A. (2008) 'The Economics of Private Equity Investments: Symposium Summary', *FRBSF Economic Letter*, San Francisco, 29 February.

Mintz, Jack M. (2007) 'Tax Competitiveness Report: A Call for Comprehensive Tax Reform', *C.D. Howe Institute Commentary*, No. 254, September: www.cdhowe.org

PME Magazine (2006) 'Le fédéralisme fiscal est un système d'avenir! – Interview with Hans-Rudolf Merz', *PME Magazine,* Geneva, October, pp. 44–6.

PME Magazine (2007) Geneva, December, pp. 57, 59.

Quitzau, Jorn (2006) *Competing Government Funding Systems* (Frankfurt am Main: Deutsche Bank Research), 12 January.

Schaaf, Jürgen (2005) *Private Equity in Europe: Buyouts Driving Growth; Start-Up Financing Drying Up* (Frankfurt am Main: Deutsche Bank Research), 26 January.

Tax Research LLP-UK (2007) *Written Submission of Evidence to the Treasury Select Committee*, prepared by Richard Murphy, FCA, July.

Teitelbaum, Richard (2007) 'The KKR Way', *Bloomberg Markets,* August, pp. 36–48.

Thornton, Emily (2007) 'Private Equity's White-Knuckle Deal', *Business Week,* 17 September.

L'Usine Nouvelle (2007) 'Transmission d'entreprise – Le tutorat en plein essor', (Transmission of Enterprises – The Coaching in Full Expansion) (Paris: *L'Usine Nouvelle*), 28 June, pp. 42–4 – in French.

Villalonga, Belén and Amit, Raphael (2004) 'How Do Family Ownership, Control, and Management Affect Firm Value?', Working paper, Wharton School/Harvard Business School, August.

Wright, M., Burrows, A., Ball, R., Scholes, L., Menteman, M. and Amess, K. (2007) *The Implications of Alternative Investment Vehicles for Corporate Governance: A Survey of Empirical Research* (Paris: OECD).

Zipfel, Frank (2007) *One Europe, One Tax? Plans for a Common Consolidated Corporate Tax Base* (Frankfurt am Main: Deutsche Bank Research), 25 September.

4
Transaction Channels and Regulatory Issues

Three notable developments increasingly characterize the PE business. First, the channels for transacting (buying or selling) have become multi-track, as this chapter attempts to show. Second, participating institutions since the 1970s have become more diverse, and their capital resources have increased considerably. Third, business owners willing to sell part or all of their enterprises have grown in number. Owners include independent entrepreneurs whose business is at an early stage of development (start-ups), family-owned businesses that need to manage successions, owners of established companies, conglomerates or industrial-trading groups that want to shed or acquire selected activities. Other reasons for such transactions include realizing attractive opportunities, concentrating on core business where management's strength is prominent, and reducing debt.

PE funds can acquire or disinvest business stakes through a variety of routes, such as: (i) organized stock exchanges which allow the acquisition of a publicly listed company, or the sale of an investee company (via initial public offering – IPO) or a portfolio of assets (via securitization); and inter-fund or trade transactions. A succinct appraisal of these approaches follows.

PE firms, before they commit capital to a target company, examine the scope of various possible avenues for future exit, even though the disinvestment is not likely to be made until three or four years from the date of the acquisition. Chief among the factors that influence the timing of an exit is the fact that the PE fund concerned has reached its mandatory end-of-life, with the legal obligation of disposing of all its investments. Another reason is that the fund's management has attained its targeted return for individual investee companies, after boosting, by use of appropriate measures, their productivity and profitability. A third reason could be that the existing PE fund does not have the resources to take one or more investee companies to the next stage of their development.

The existence of multiple exit options characterized by rapid or easy disposal of PE funds' investments enhances the funds' liquidity and performance (measured by the IRR, DCF, or multiples of EBIT or EBITAD). Such exit options help to attract investors' capital to the PE sector, and promote the funding of businesses in need of capital.

Stock exchanges

Sizeable and developed organized capital markets help PE firms' activities in two major respects. They allow PE firms to:

(a) acquire the listed shares of targeted companies and convert them into private, non-listed companies, to be managed or supervised by a team nominated by the PE firm; PE firms negotiate in parallel the conversion of investee companies' tradable debt instruments into private debt held by lending institutions; and
(b) sell their portfolio companies to the general public of investors, through IPO operations launched on stock exchanges at a timely moment.

The strategy of acquiring publicly-listed companies is carried out generally with the approval of the targeted company's board of directors and top management. It is nevertheless possible for a PE firm to approach shareholders in the company directly (that is, to make a hostile bid), if the company's board refuses to discuss a deal (see, for example, *Financial Times*, 2007).

Efficient organization, operation and regulation of stock exchanges are vital for attracting the general public of investors, enhancing financial stability and protecting against potential abuses. Among regulatory principles, several stock exchanges require that the company proposed for an IPO has a responsible management, a 'reasonable' performance (for example, profits over a couple of years preceding the public offer), regular transparent reporting of its accounts (usually on a quarterly basis), and non-discriminatory treatment of potential investors.

The GP of the PE fund can resort to (i) the sale of individual portfolio companies to third-party investors by IPO; and/or (ii) the distribution of newly issued stocks of the companies to members of the LP. Stocks distributed to the latter are subject to the restriction of a 'holding period' and cannot be sold freely in the market – except after a certain period, since the PE fund is legally considered to be an *insider*, because of its significant ownership/managerial role in the company under IPO. Regulation and underwriting agreements generally bar the all insiders from liquidating their allotted IPO stocks of such a company before the expiration of a specific lock-in period (which may extend over several months).

Investment bankers often act as vendors of businesses on behalf of owners. They set the share price of a private client company going public (IPO), and arrange for the placement of the company's shares among investors (institutional and private). In the placement of shares, an investment bank (or a syndicate of investment banks) can resort to a 'best effort' approach. Alternatively, the investment bank agrees with its client company to underwrite the sale of IPO shares, whereby it accepts a 'firm commitment' to buy unsold shares at pre-agreed prices. The latter approach often justifies sizeable underwriting fees (varying between 7 per cent for medium-sized flotations, and 4 per cent for the largest ones). In an IPO operation, the contribution of an investment banking institution to the selling party comes essentially in organizing the mobilization of investors and creditors, including deciding on optimal *pricing* of IPO stocks and *timing* of the initial launch. Should the capital market's developments turn unattractive, the IPO launchers need to reschedule that operation.

IPOs can also be constrained by the absence of recognized security exchanges or automated quotation systems, as well as by the lack of interest among investors. Thus the effective closing of the *Neuer Markt* in 2002 hurt Germany's venture capital/private equity markets – following an investors' withdrawal from the market after the crash of a wide range of information technology (IT) companies. As such, the closure may have constrained the funding of innovative FBs/SMEs.

Compared to sizeable and well-established companies, which have had ready access to world-class public markets for many years, smaller growing private companies (from developed and emerging economies) can nowadays tap increasingly into a variety of organized markets for IPOs, such as the Alternative Investment Market (AIM) on the London Stock Exchange (LSE). Known for its simplicity and flexibility, AIM does not stipulate minimum size, track record, minimum number of shares in public hands or market capitalization. Since November 2007, the LSE has furthermore facilitated the listing of investment firms (PE funds and hedge funds) by unifying the listing regime (in lieu of a two-tier listing regime with lighter rules for non-British funds) in a Specialist Fund Market, in competition with rival exchanges (such as the New York Stock Exchange, and Euronext in Amsterdam).

In the absence of organized stock exchange markets, electronic over-the-counter (OTC) transaction of shares has become available. US regulations require the companies concerned to have at least forty shareholders and full reporting to the Securities and Exchange Commission (SEC). The OTC alternative – compared to the IPO – is financially attractive in so far as the cumulative fees for going down this route are lower (see Gustke, 2005). The regulatory requirements of reporting to the SEC (or similar bodies) for IPO or OTC transactions are deemed acceptable by investors who are wary of abuse. Thus the London Stock Exchange has become an attractive venue for investments in companies originating in countries where no IPO outlets exist. This is often done through bank certificates known as *global depository receipts* (GDRs), which are foreign-listed instruments representing shares (see, for example, *The Economist*, 2006a).

Inter-fund and trade transactions

Transactions among PE funds, referred to as 'secondary markets', have become an important exit route. It is common to find a PE fund selling a portfolio company to another PE fund. This is often the case when the buying PE fund has the talent and the financial resources to boost further the development of the targeted company. Another reason could be that the selling PE fund is faced with mandatory legal obligations of winding-up its fund by a fixed date.

Some PE funds also specialize in buying out limited partners' interests in other funds. The LP seeks generally, for reasons of liquidity or change in strategy, to sell his/her interests to firms that specialize in PE secondary assets before the expiration date of a limited partnership fund. Such transactions, prior to the contractual end of a PE fund's life, require the consent of the GP that had set up the fund.

Before the completion of the above-mentioned sale transaction, the other LP members of the fund concerned have – in principle – the right of first refusal. The buyer, from within or outside the PE fund, then assumes all the rights and obligations of the seller.

The sale price of a PE investment can be negotiated discreetly and bilaterally between buyer and seller. Alternatively, the investment may be open to competitive bidding. Key factors influencing the auction price level are the size of financial resources seeking investment, the number of bidders, the number of investment deals available in the market, and expectations of return on these investments reflecting various influences, such as market exuberance or market pessimism (see Friedlander, 2004).

The seller of a business needs to minimize the disclosure of proprietary information, and the bidders want to minimize their expenses (for example, those relating to their investigations) in respect of the potential attractiveness of the deal proposed. In a second phase, after screening and selecting serious and eligible buying candidates, the vendor can provide the chosen PE fund(s) and other potential buyers with additional information on the company for sale. In the final stage, confidential information will be disclosed solely to the chosen bidder who demonstrates a genuine interest and has the capacity to realize the transaction. The finalist obtains an exclusivity period to carry out his/her due diligence after committing to a purchase price within parameters set by a 'letter of intent' issued by the prospective buyer and agreed to by the seller, (see also Bank of America, 2003). The 'fair value' of a privately held company can be as much as 30 per cent below that of a comparable listed company, for reasons of illiquidity and relative opacity (see www.cavendish.com).

PE funds deal importantly with industrial trading groups which (a) spin-off or de-merge their non-core units that are impeding their profit growth; or (b) buy companies that contribute to boosting their earnings. Their acquisitions are notably prompted by:

(a) achieving economies of size or scope and diversifying risks;
(b) creating synergies or complementarities (for example, through vertical or horizontal integrations) with their other core activities;
(c) rationalizing support facilities (for example, back-office functions, human resources, information systems, procurement, marketing);

(d) obtaining a rapid expansion in another market – instead of relying on the slow process of building that expansion from within the firm; and
(e) pre-empting a strategic positioning (by reference to innovation, technology, market leadership or other factors) *vis-à-vis* competitors (see, for example, O'Sullivan, 2006).

For the above-mentioned reasons, the sale of a company to a trading/industrial group commands a premium, compared to a sale to a financial buyer such as a PE firm. The latter has a limited time horizon for adding value to a portfolio company (typically some five years) before selling the company. By comparison, the trading/industrial group is not constrained by such a limited time horizon and can invest over a longer period of time.

Compared to financial acquirers, an industrial/commercial group has to be attentive to certain challenges. Among these, one should mention (a) the delays created by clearance procedures from the antitrust authorities, which are concerned about concentrated markets limiting competition (these authorities could impose difficult measures – such as the obligation to sever or spin-off some significant activities of the acquired business); and (b) the problem of achieving a rapid and smooth integration of the acquired entity within the purchasing group. Successful integration involves sustaining the motivation, efficiency and creativity of human resources; expanding the customer base; maintaining beneficial relations with suppliers, subcontractors and others. Financial buyers do not usually face antitrust reviews, unless they have other portfolio companies within the same business sector.

Securitization of PE portfolios

For major operations in disposing of business stakes, one can refer to Deutsche Bank, which was a pioneer in 2003 with the sale of €1.502 billion of assets through *management buyouts* (see Deutsche Bank press release, 21 February 2003), the *direct sale* of US$400 million of its private equity investments to a specialized PE fund (Crédit Suisse Strategic Partners) and the *securitization* of a portfolio of US$467 million it held in private equity (see, for the latter two operations: Deutsche Bank press release, 1 August 2003).

Financial or non-financial groups can create off-balance-sheet legal entities that pool selected categories of assets to back securities for sale to investors through the issue of negotiable collateralized debt obligations (CDOs). Securitization can apply to a wide spectrum of asset classes. These include, in particular: commercial and residential properties and mortgages, auto loans and leases, credit card receivables, trade receivables, student loans, equipment loans and leases (relating to aircraft, vessels, rail cars, containers, computers, construction equipment, and others), insurance premiums, mezzanine finance, private senior or subordinated debt, governmental debt, distressed loans, private equity and a variety of hybrid assets. Securitization of PE interests is a nascent market of comparatively moderate importance.

Three major steps are involved in the securitization process: (i) the sale of a class of assets (debt or equity) to a special purpose vehicle (SPV), which is supposed to be insulated from the risks of default by the originator/vendor of the assets; (ii) the issue of negotiable securities (such as CDOs) backed by the assets held by the SPV; and (iii) the sale to investors of the issued securities. The value of the securities and their yield is related directly to the value and risks of the pooled class of assets, as determined by (a) the size and reliability of expected future cash flows they are likely to generate; and (b) credit enhancement techniques attached to these securities, such as equity or guarantees provided by prime-rated entities, which commit to absorb the first eventual losses incurred by the SPV. These securities are made available to a wide circle of investors (mainly institutional).

Subject to a sound and effective regulatory framework, securitization can offer several benefits to various parties concerned in a PE fund. In particular, it

(i) provides the original PE fund's investors with the opportunity of liquidity;
(ii) spares the PE investor in need of liquidity the eventuality of having to bear a steep discount associated with a forced sale of his/her PE rights to another investor;
(iii) opens-up for the general public of investors (who do not normally buy PE stakes directly) instruments backed by PE assets;
(iv) widens the category of asset types for investors seeking diversification of risks and returns; and

(v) Increases the mobility of capital and moderates its cost in the national economies concerned thanks to greater liquidity, more diversification of risks, and greater competition among participants.

Major functions in the securitization process of PE interests are listed in Exhibit 4.1. For PE funds organized as 'limited partnerships' – a prevalent type – the securitization operation starts with a consent agreement between the LP (the original investors) and the GP who are responsible for the management of the investors' fund.

Until recently, PE interests outside the real estate rental sector were not readily amenable to securitization because of the high uncertainty of predicting cash flows and the lumpiness of income accruing from the PE portfolio of companies (usually generated after a number of years in the form of capital gains).

The securitization agreement – subject to the consent of all parties concerned – specifies the terms of the transfer of the rights and responsibilities of PE investors to an independently managed 'bankruptcy-remote' special purpose vehicle (SPV). The SPV would then become the basis on which asset-backed securities will be issued for sale to investors. The valuation of interests transferred has to be made by an independent institution acceptable to the credit rating agencies. The latter are accredited by the SEC as NRSROs (Nationally Recognized Statistical Rating Organizations). Nevertheless, credit rating agencies are not legally liable for their ratings (considered 'opinions' protected by the First Amendment of the US Constitution) and are immune to civil or criminal liability for malfeasance (see Partnoy, 2006).

To appeal to a wide spectrum of investors – mostly institutional – with differing risk/reward appetites, the 'tranching' method is used. This method stratifies the issued securities by apportioning the SPV's cash flows: riskless bond-like *super-senior* investment-grade classes of securities (AAA) earn significantly lower interest rates than *junior* tranches of securities, which absorb eventual losses. Junior tranches are generally held by the sponsors or residual owners of the SPV.

The risk factor can be linked directly to the absence of regular predictable cash flows and the lumpiness of income accruing mainly in the form of expected capital gains, realized upon the sale of investments held by the SPV. In such a situation of irregular and

Exhibit 4.1 Key functions in the securitization process of PE portfolios

1. Origination, structuring, and legal registration of the special purpose vehicle (SPV).
2. Sponsors' memorandum to investors defining the nights and obligations of transferors, transferees and the SVP's management.
3. Valuation of the SVP's assets and of its collateralized debt obligations (CDOs).
4. Risk mitigation through: (a) selection of the SVP's assets; (b) 'liquidity facility' to honour financial charges on time; (c) underwriting or guarantee of CDOs; (d) over-collateralization of the CDOs; (e) credit enhancements; (f) subordinated debt; and (f) equity first-loss tranche.
5. Credit rating of securities (CDOs).
6. Issuance and placement of securities with investors.
7. Servicing all parties to the SPV: registration, accounting, reporting to investors and rating agencies, arbitrage and hedging operations, redemption, and others.

See also D'Souza, 2003; and Deutsche Bank's Annual Reports and press releases.

unpredictable cash flows, the financial structuring of the SPV would imperatively require the creation of a 'liquidity facility' that can meet contingencies of temporary shortages of cash. That cash cushion is needed to meet on time mandatory debt servicing (payment of interest and/or principal) on the investment grade debt notes bought-up by third-party investors.

Rating agencies, with full access to key data on the investments held by the SPV and with historical evidence available on comparable funds, can measure likely potential cash shortages – by resorting to scenarios of stress testing. Concomitantly, the agencies would determine the optimal capital structure of the SPV, its various debt tranches, and its liquidity facility. Rating CDOs based on tranched pools of credit exposures call for the triple exercise of (i) attributing a probability of default to each obligor within the pool; (ii) estimating default correlations among individual collateral assets within the pool; and (iii) estimating recovery rates of assets in total or partial default. This calls for designing realistic models – whose hypotheses need to be fine-tuned to new conditions as they unfold. However, the credit agencies' models had been occasionally flawed (for example, when they rated bonds backed by dubious mortgage loans over 2002–2007; see Chapter 1).

The SPV sponsors and beneficial owners would normally subscribe to all the non-rated equity/first loss tranche and the subordinated debt tranche. The senior (presumed to be largely insulated from default risk) and other low-risk notes are left to third-party investors. The sponsors' stake in the SPV capital could well vary between 25 per cent and 50 per cent of the total capital structure – according to the above-mentioned Deutsche Bank source (the bank resorted to sizeable sales and securitization operations of its PE investments over the period 2002–4). The exact percentage is influenced by two important factors: (a) the higher the risk of the underlying investment portfolio, the higher the percentage of capital taken by the sponsors; and (b) the higher the aversion of general 'market sentiment' to risk-taking, the higher the said percentage.

Potential investors in the above-mentioned securitized SPVs are essentially institutions that command sizeable financial resources. They include insurance companies, pension funds, hedge funds and banks. In the pursuit of fiscal optimization, the SPVs are generally based in 'tax-friendly' jurisdictions whose reputation regarding controls over money laundering and integrity-prudential matters is acceptable to the regulatory authorities of the PE fund's home country.

Challenges of PE securitization

Notwithstanding the existence of a sound regulatory framework, the implementation of a PE fund's securitization programme raises a number of contentious issues, especially in limited partnerships. These issues comprise notably:

(i) the lack of high-quality collateralized assets and the absence of a balanced diversification of risks needed to protect holders of 'senior debt notes';

(ii) the cost, complexity and long lead time required to prepare the securitization operation;
(iii) the PE fund's GP and LP have to agree on assets to be transferred to the SPV, and on a tax-friendly domicile acceptable to the regulatory authorities of the PE fund's home country;
(iv) the soundness of accounting standards used in the valuation of PE assets transferred to the SPV; and
(v) the propensity issuers have to *shop around* for rating agencies whose CDO models appear to favour them (see Fender and Kiff, 2004).

In order to facilitate the raising of funds from public markets, the securities offered for public subscription should be properly rated by accredited agencies recognized by the regulatory authorities – taking into consideration the value of the collateral pool, and the credit-worthiness of the issuer and underwriters (see, for example, Packer *et al.*, 2007). The three major credit rating agencies, listed by date of establishment, are Moody's, Standard & Poor's, and Fitch – the first two being the biggest.

Queries are raised from several quarters regarding occasional loose oversight exercised by the regulatory authorities (such as, the Securities and Exchange Commission (SEC) in the USA) over the credit rating industry, and the oligopolistic market structure and behaviour of that industry – leading to hefty fees charged to issuers, the publication of unsolicited ratings that could put pressure on issuers to pay them fees, and their active marketing of ancillary consulting services – all creating situations of potential conflict of interest (see, for example: Partnoy, 2006; also *The Economist*, 2005b, 2007e). Spokespersons for the credit rating agencies have staunchly defended the quality of their credit rating methodologies, their track record of objectivity, and their independence *vis-à-vis* issuers who pay for their services (see, for example, Tillman, 2003). Several episodes have, however, shown a lack of knowledge, professional rigour or foresight on the part of a number of parties involved in the process of the evaluation of financial instruments: this includes credit rating agencies which over-rated financial instruments – for example, those of the subprime mortgages, generating the world-wide crisis of 2006–9 (see, for example, Tomlinson and Evans, 2007; Evans, 2007; and Stuart, 2008).

Possibly the major problem with securitization of PE portfolios relates to the regulatory disclosure of significant, detailed and accurate information (often required on a quarterly basis) and their dissemination to a large number of actual and potential investors and other market players interested in the instruments issued by the SPV. Furthermore, the composition of these investors is in continuous flux, in so far as securities issued by the SPV do change hands in active trading. For PE funds, information on their acquired companies is considered largely confidential and proprietary. The disclosure of proprietary information to a wide spectrum of third parties linked to the securitization operation could have an adverse effect on the fund's performance.

One should stress that the operation of securitization calls for the clear allocation of rights and obligations between the transferor and the transferee, as well as their strict observation. These include accepting long-term liability associated with 'claw back' clauses, defraying of management services, follow-up on honouring capital commitments, payment of outstanding management fees, anticipated fund expenses for the transfer operation, and others (see, for example, Cohen and Aiello, 2004; available at: www.weil.com). The transferee – given the foregoing requirements – is likely to require a lower price related to the fair value of the equity stake under negotiation.

The liquidity solution obtained through securitization can also present certain risks for investee companies. In particular, it could encourage the flow of unstable funds to the PE sector. By opening-up to 'hot money', the PE sector (normally in need of stable funds to nurture investee companies over a few years) would face increased volatility. This view was expressed eloquently by experienced PE researchers thus: 'As [PE] funds become more liquid, there is more danger that they will attract financially unstable investors, which may lead to greater difficulties in raising new funds' (see Lerner and Schoar, 2004).

Hedge funds and private equity

One needs to underline the critical importance of long duration of invested capital in the promotion of entrepreneurial (notably start-ups) and high growth businesses. Indeed, such business activities may take several years before they come to full fruition. The typical PE fund holds its investments 'long' in illiquid assets (e.g. acquired companies) over a multi-year time horizon, with business strategies aimed at realizing their high potential. Unlike PE funds, the cutting edge expertise of hedge funds is not in the management of companies, but rather in actively trading financial instruments and other reasonably liquid assets – exploiting particularly market inefficiencies and pricing anomalies. Their investments are essentially in marketable instruments, generally held over very short periods (stretching from hours to a few weeks). Hedge funds are thus likely to attract talents capable of (a) trading in liquid securities, taking both 'long' and 'short' positions; and (b) structuring and trading in derivatives and other sophisticated financial products. Their managers' mindset, skills and experiences are generally geared to current or short-term opportunities in financial markets. They are not concerned by the legal constraints of insider information – to the extent they are not involved in the management of companies whose securities they trade.

Hedge funds, in comparison to PE funds, have therefore much shorter holding periods since they have to honour investors' redemption rights. Generally, lock-up periods of hedge funds hover around one month to one quarter of a year. A few hedge funds have tried to improve lacklustre returns by investing in private equity with up to three-year lock-ins. Indeed, statistical data show, for the period 2003–6, that hedge funds with a one-month redemption period had returns of about 15 per cent on average to investors, while those with one-year lock-ins returned more than 30 per cent to investors (see Baddepudi, 2006). In 2007, hedge fund allocated an estimated 10 to 20 percent of their resources for illiquid assets (see, for example, *Hedge Fund Manger Week*, 2007).

Hedge funds investments in PE stakes are limited (less than 30 per cent of total net assets under their management). The stakes can nevertheless be substantial in absolute terms. To address that challenge, hedge funds could (a) limit their investors' redemption right to the liquid portion of their portfolio; (b) create alongside their hedge funds separate PE vehicles; or (c) create 'side pockets' in their accounts to cater for their illiquid assets, such as PE stakes, real estate and loans (see, for example, Saffayeh and Lotem, 2005/6).

Sizeable PE firms have similarly moved into the territory of hedge funds, prompted essentially by two motives: first, their wish to manage profitably large proceeds accruing from exiting an investee company or a portfolio of such companies pending their setting up a new PE fund; and second, the objective of building-up a pool of capital that can readily be drawn upon (practically without delay) as and when PE opportunities arise and require debt leveraging – without having to resort to time-consuming (and possibly onerous) borrowing from banks.

Since the banking sector is closely regulated, PE funds have of late sought and obtained for their buyouts large volumes of private funding from the lightly regulated hedge funds – to avoid mandatory transparency *vis-à-vis* regulators or markets, and thus avoid their monitoring and scrutiny (see, for example, Geithner, 2006; and *The Economist*, 2006c).

PE firms' credibility *vis-à-vis* entrepreneurs and business sellers can be enhanced considerably if they have a pool of capital at hand to draw on for investment or lending. Moreover, a financial group managing a range of activities (PE funds, hedge funds, other pools of capital, M&A services and so on) under one corporate roof would protect its client base and provide its investors with the opportunity to diversify their investments in-house. Otherwise, investors in limited lifespan PE funds, once they recoup their capital and gains, might decide to invest it with other financial groups that offer them a variety of capital pools. To appeal to investors with differing profiles and objectives, a financial group would offer investment vehicles focused on different investment strategies (with reference to sectors, time horizons, geographic spread, risk/return levels, liquidity, and other criteria).

Whither PE performance?

PE firms comprise a wide spectrum of business groups whose performance varies considerably. Superior performance was reportedly limited to a few: only the top twenty-five well-established private equity firms among some 1,000 PE firms (see *The Economist*, 2004b). In obtaining attractive deals, the performing firms have capitalized on their track records of achievements and business relations cultivated over several year – compared to newcomers.

PE firms may underperform for multiple reasons, covering micro factors (such as poor choice of investee companies, inefficient oversight or management of these companies, or excessive debt leveraging) or macro factors (such as recession, political or economic instability, and environmental problems). Such factors could well lead to losses thereby affecting adversely PE firms' capacity to attract investors' capital. The Centre for Management Buy-Out Research at Nottingham University has reported statistics on PE buy-outs in the United Kingdom market since 1991. Its figures show that, on average, close to a third of investee companies in British PE firms' portfolios have failed on exit (see www.cmbor.com).

PE firms are naturally weary of the 'reputation cost' that is generated by the negative publicity of the bankruptcy of one or more of their portfolio companies, thereby hurting their chances of attracting investors. They are also concerned about the possible need for expensive talents and large financial resources to be devoted to the rescue of such companies. They may even not be equipped in terms of internal skills to handle such situations. Finally, they may find the waiting period for revitalizing a portfolio company too long for a fixed-time PE fund, as agreed with investors. In these circumstances, a PE firm's management often prefers to sell such PE stakes (even at *dumped* prices) rather than to continue being burdened by holding problematic investments that could sour even further – leading to a possible substantial drain on the PE firm's human and financial resources, with protracted litigations and court proceedings.

A PE firm's sale of a poorly performing portfolio company at a loss – in the absence of internal expertise to turn it around – is better than bearing the 'reputation risk' resulting from an eventual bankrupt investee company. For funds investing with high-risk industries (for example, turnaround companies or start-ups), investment managers are expected, along with their collaborators, to devote more time to hands-on management, and eventually recruit outside specialists for the turnaround. Some PE funds specialize in distressed assets and shop for 'opportunities' among business entities under receivership (such as the so-called 'Chapter 11' companies). Managers of such funds should have proven skills for *turning around* failed companies, and their investors may be willing to assume the risks attendant on such investments, expecting attractive returns from revitalized companies. Companies under receivership can be bought up from bankruptcy courts at the liquidation value of their assets, which may be priced at *fire-sale* levels.

Competent turnaround management can transform distressed companies from potential wrecks into 'going concerns' – through downsizing the business by weeding out unprofitable operations in order to consolidate the most profitable parts. Such turnaround management would call for painful measures *vis-à-vis* certain stakeholders (notably in the form of wiping-up equity and debt, discontinuation of activities, reduced employment, and/or lower salaries) in expectation of reviving the failed company (see, for example, *The Economist*, 2007b).

Private versus publicly-listed companies

While investment firms have the possibility of being exempt from disclosing information if they are legally organized as 'private companies', a few have gone down the public-listing route, thereby accepting disclosure and reporting requirements. This has been the case with a few European and American PE firms. Despite the fact that listing requirements have become more stringent since the Sarbanes–Oxley Act of 2002, the management company of the Blackstone Group – one of the world's largest 'alternative investments' enterprise – has chosen to list in the USA with a partial IPO (about 10 per cent of its capital, estimated at some US$4 billion), carried out on 22 June 2007. The partial IPO of Blackstone's PE management firm – as a publicly traded partnership (the earlier example in the USA is Fortress Investment Group) – does not cover stakes in investee companies (see Form S-1 as filed with the SEC by The Blackstone Group L.P. on 22 March 2007). On 21 May 2007, Blackstone agreed to sell an additional US$3 billion non-voting shares (roughly an 8 per cent stake) to the state-owned China Investment Corporation. The latter agreed to keep its stake for at least four years (and with the constraint of divesting after that period not more than US$1 billion per year), and not to invest in a competing PE firm for a year.

Several reasons prompted Blackstone's owners early in 2007 to list publicly their management firm of financial pools of 'alternative investments' through the sale of a portion of their equity to outsiders. The first was to cash out part of the value of their firm's accomplishments at a timely 'high phase' of the PE cycle. A second reason was that existing partners will not lose control of their enterprise (since the new shareholders will be a 'minority', with limited voting power and no right to elect board members or to decide on executives' compensation). A third reason for the partial IPO could well be to raise from financial markets additional permanent capital to finance future expansion. A fourth motivation for a minority public listing is to prove to incoming shareholders that the existing majority owners have full confidence in the future of their enterprise, in so far as they are retaining a large majority in the capital. A fifth motivation, with respect to the sale to China, is Blackstone's objective of accessing the booming business opportunities in the Chinese market.

Publicly-listed companies are under the legal obligation of disclosing periodically (annually, semi-annually or quarterly) to their shareholders, the general public of investors and the regulatory authorities detailed and comprehensive information on their assets, profits, strategies and compensation of executives. PE funds – in so far as they are organized as 'privately-held non-regulated business entities' – deem such information to belong to the domain of proprietary rights, to be shielded from competitors and the general public. As such, PE firms' transparency of information on their portfolios of private companies is limited or brief – compared to publicly-listed companies. This explains, *inter alia*, PE management's strategy of de-listing, immediately upon their acquisition, hitherto publicly-listed companies. Not only are shares de-listed, but also publicly-held and traded debt would be converted into bilaterally negotiated debt with individual financial institutions or with syndicates of the latter.

A few senior executives of publicly-listed companies have favoured working for companies in the PE sector. Their preference stems from their wish to avoid compliance with transparency and other requirements set up by laws, regulations and corporate governance codes for publicly-listed companies (see, for example, Weir, 2006). Some fiercely opposing shareholders of these companies have accused their management of conniving with the interested PE firm: they argue that 'they are selling too cheaply in order to get a bigger slice of the profits for themselves when the private-equity buyer eventually sells the firm' later on (*The Economist,* 2007a). One may relate the foregoing to the fact that 'the most successful private equity partners can earn several times the salary of a chief executive running a FTSE 100 company' (see *The Independent,* 2007). Public reporting and disclosure requirements do not apply to the activities of PE firms, including the compensation packages of their PE executives. Even GP disclosures to LP (pension funds and other institutional investors, endowments, wealthy families, and others) are succinct. PE executives are nevertheless concerned about pressures that could come from investors, trade unions and political quarters.

For publicly-traded companies, transparency rules on total compensation packages for named executive officers and three additional employees with policy-making functions, introduced by the US Securities and Exchange Commission (SEC) in 2006, are comprehensive. They cover regular salary, benefits worth more than US$10,000 (previously above US$50,000), the timing and fair value of stocks and stock-options grants (including dividends and gains), pay to executives on severance or change of control of the company, retirement pension, and other benefits. All these components (the current, and the future or contingent) must be duly filed annually with the SEC (subject to the CEO and CFO certifications as required by the Sarbanes–Oxley Act – SOX) and presented in a standardized clear and direct language understandable by the unsophisticated lay investor, and comparable from company to company. The SEC has left it to the board of directors' compensation committee, and ultimately the corporation's shareholders of individual companies, to decide on the 'right' level of an executive's compensation and the need to set limits (see 'Speech by SEC Chairman Christopher Cox', 26 July 2006; executive compensation for the companies concerned are available at: www.sec.gov).

The above-mentioned disclosures exclude key employees who may be getting substantial rewards, on the apparent grounds that they are not involved in managerial functions. They also exclude the fees received by compensation consultants. The latter have a conflict of interest and duties in advising on executives' pay packages, without disclosing the fees they receive for their consultancy in this respect. Moreover, these consultants, with the extra data at their disposal, could advise boards to raise the pay of executives and policy-making officers to match their highest-paid peers (see, for example, US House of Representatives, Committee on Oversight and Government Reform, 2007; also Clark, 2006).

Corporate boards, ostensibly acting on behalf of shareholders, could well be 'captured or partially captured by management' when setting executive compensation (see literature cited by Kuhnen and Zweibel, 2007). Informed analysts deem the SOX disclosure rules on executives' compensation packages adopted by the SEC to be *ineffective*, in so far as the voting system does not allow shareholders to oust directors whose pay is deemed to be *excessive* (the latter qualification is, albeit, difficult to ascertain), or unrelated to their effective contribution in the enterprise's performance. Moreover, the SEC rules 'do not address the problem of big rewards for failure, which provide such a dangerous incentive for chief executive officers to bet the company' and adopt excessively risky strategies with impunity (see Plender, 2006). US Congressional hearings have disclosed, on the basis of subpoenaed witnesses and internal corporate documents, outrageous bonuses being paid to executives, despite meagre returns or crushing losses being sustained by their firms. This was admitted, for example, in the testimony of Richard S. Fuld, Jr. the CEO of Lehman Brothers, an erstwhile prestigious investment bank, which filed for bankruptcy in September 2008. It appears that executives had clung to their bonuses despite the bank's devastating losses (see Hearings on 'Causes and Effects of Lehman Brothers Bankruptcy' at the House Oversight Committee on 6 October 2008; available at: http://oversight.house.gov).

Experience has shown that self-regulation is not sufficient to avoid possible abuses by management and to protect various stakeholders' interests. Executives are generally lured by personal material *gain*. 'Accountability for failure' should, therefore, be an integral part of the compensation packages of executives, with pay contracts including 'claw-back' clauses for non-performance during their period of responsibility.

Moreover, self-regulation is not capable of controlling collusion – as was reported regarding US financial analysts recommending stocks to investors in return for favours from the management of the companies concerned (see Westphal and Clement, 2007; also Box 4.1). Such inappropriate behaviours have been revealed by regulatory authorities (see, for example, the investigations of the New York State Attorney General in 2002; also *The Economist*, 2004a and 2007d). Concerned about their reputation, managers should beaware of such practices.

To avoid conflicts of interest and unfair trading, more rigorous and effective control systems to prevent abuse or fraud and to ensure the truthfulness of accounts have been introduced *vis-à-vis* listed companies' management and their auditors. This is notably the case with the tougher penalties currently applicable in the USA (Sarbanes–Oxley

Box 4.1 Conflicts of interest – an example
Federal court approves settlement of SEC enforcement actions involving conflicts of interest between research and investment banking

Washington, DC, October 31, 2003 – The Securities and Exchange Commission announced today that the Honorable William H. Pauley III, United States District Judge for the Southern District of New York, approved the $1.4 billion global settlement of enforcement actions against ten of the nation's top investment firms and two associated individuals. The enforcement actions alleged undue influence of investment banking interests on securities research at brokerage firms. The enforcement actions and the proposed settlements were announced on April 28, 2003. In addition to entering the Order approving the global settlement, the Court also entered orders as to certain of the firms relating to the Distribution Funds and the Investor Education Fund. These orders provide further details as to investors who may be eligible to receive proceeds from the Distribution Funds to be created as part of the global settlement and set forth a framework for a non-profit organization to fund worthy and cost-efficient investor education programs. The Court also entered separate Final Judgments as to each of the 12 defendants.

SEC Chairman William H. Donaldson said, 'The Commission is pleased that the Court, after having conducted a thorough review of the proposed global settlement, has approved the settlement and found it to be in the public interest. We now begin the process of implementing the settlement, which we believe is an important part of our ongoing efforts to restore investors' faith in the fairness and integrity of our markets.' Under the terms of the Final Judgments and Orders that Judge Pauley approved today, the ten firms and two individuals will pay a total of $894 million in penalties and disgorgement, consisting of $397 million in disgorgement and $497 million in penalties, which includes one firm's previous payment of $100 million in connection with its prior settlement with the states.

The Final Judgments also require the firms to make payments totalling $432.5 million to fund independent research for investors. Seven of the firms will make payments of $80 million to fund and promote investor education. In addition to the monetary payments, the firms are required to undertake dramatic reforms to their future practices, including separating their research and investment banking departments.

Source: US Securities and Exchange Commission, whose archives are openly available electronically at www.sec.gov.

Act) which require the top management of listed companies to certify financial results, subject to official sanctions for corporate abuses, eventually leading to penal prosecution by the regulatory authorities and class-action law suits (see also *The Economist*, 2005a).

The above-mentioned regulations tend to make the management of publicly-listed companies (whether in the financial or non-financial sectors) cautious and thus risk averse – in so far as a company's management that makes an error is heavily punished by the regulatory authorities, and the shares of the company concerned will be consequently sanctioned by the market. In these circumstances, certain managers prefer working for PE firms in order to remain out of the limelight (see, for example, *Financial Times*, 2004; and *The Economist*, 2006b).

Decrying regulatory measures at the time they are imposed may be an unbalanced judgement. A sober evaluation would require adequate experience over a reasonably long stretch of time. Thus, the Sarbanes–Oxley Act (intended to apply rigorous corporate accountability, transparent financial reporting, and criminal liability for executives blamed for grave dereliction of duty) proved onerous during its first year of implementation. Subsequently, it has become less costly and has provided valuable insights for management, enabling them to improve efficiency. The Act has improved corporate organization and controls, reduced operational risks and losses and reduced shareholder value (see Wagner and Dittmar, 2006).

Other researchers have estimated that the Act's costs have been especially burdensome for smaller companies, and have undermined the entrepreneurial risk-taking spirit in the USA. It has discouraged foreign firms from listing on US stock exchanges, and facilitated the de-listing of sizeable companies whose top management has thus been induced to co-operate with PE acquirers, prompted by lucrative incentives of sharing in capital gains (see *The Economist,* 2007c; links to various papers and reports used by the article can be accessed at: www.economist.com/sarbanes-oxleysources).

PE transactions have multiple avenues for their realization – as presented in this chapter. The choice of one avenue in preference to others is often *opportunistic,* and depends on market conditions and potential gains expected at the time the parties concerned conclude their transaction. While it is desirable to prepare carefully for an optimal 'transaction avenue', it may prove difficult always to realize expectations with respect to that avenue in a dynamic environment. Nevertheless, PE managers, and their investment bankers, may well be advised to anticipate, and to have contingency plans ready – should events move in unforseen directions. One such plan consists of selling in an orderly transaction the remaining assets (which could not be easily disposed of in the market and after netting related liabilities) to one or more of the fund's willing investors, at their estimated *fair value* (equivalent to an arm's length sale to a third party). The PE firm could conceivably also sell the above-mentioned remaining assets to a new PE fund it has arranged to launch.

References

Baddepudi, Rajeev (2006) 'Key Trends in European Hedge Funds', *Hedge Fund Monthly,* Eurkahedge, June – cited in *Financial Times Weekly Review of the Investment Industry,* 31 July, p. 2.

Bank of America (2003) 'Protecting Against 'Re-trading' in the Private M&A Auction', by Robert Seber, *CapitalEyes,* December.

Clark, Hannah (2006) 'Will Threat of Disclosure Keep Lid on Pay?', *Forbes,* 26 July.

Cohen, Paul and Aiello, John (2004) 'Secondary Investing in Private Equity Funds: Primary Issues for General Partners', Weil, Gotshal & Manges, international law firm, 28 January.

D'Souza, Jeffrey (2003) 'Private Equity Securitisation', Deutsche Bank.

Economist, The (2004a) 'Google's IPO – A Cartel-buster', 8 May, p. 14.

Economist, The (2004b) 'Kings of Capitalism – A Survey of Private Equity', 27 November, p. 6.

Economist, The (2005a) 'Foreign Listings in New York – Big Apple Blues', 29 January, p. 69.

Economist, The (2005b) 'Who Rates the Raters?', 26 March, pp. 65–7.

Economist, The (2006a) 'Russian IPOs', 28 January, pp. 73–4.

Economist, The (2006b) 'Pay and Private Equity – The Benefits of Privacy', 18 March, p. 63.

Economist, The (2006c) 'In the Shadows of Debt', 23 September, pp. 69–72.

Economist, The (2007a) 'The Uneasy Crown', 10 February, pp. 14–15 and 73–5.

Economist, The (2007b) 'Investing in Distress – The Vultures Take Wing', 31 March, pp. 77–80.

Economist, The (2007c) 'Sarbanes–Oxley – Five Years Under the Thumb', 28 July, pp. 65–6.

Economist, The (2007d) 'Equity Research – Trading Favours' 28 July, pp. 70–1.

Economist, The (2007e) 'Credit and Blame – The Rating Agencies Operate on Shaky Foundations', 8 September, p. 72.

Evans, David (2007) 'The Poison in Your Pension', *Bloomberg Markets*, July, pp. 36–70.

Fender, Ingo and Kiff, John (2004) *CDO Rating Methodology: Some Thoughts on Model Risk and its Implications*, BIS Working Papers No. 163, Bank for International Settlements, November.

Financial Times (2004) 'New Rules "Putting Pressure on Companies to Go Private"', 14 May, p. 15.

Financial Times (2007) 'CVC Investors Give Their Approval for Hostile Bids', 2 January, p. 16.

Friedlander, Josh (2004) 'Why Private Equity Firms May Overpay to Win Auctions', *CapitalEyes*, Bank of America, November, pp. 5–7.

Geithner, Timothy F., President and CEO, Federal Reserve Bank of New York (2006) 'Hedge Funds and Derivatives and Their Implications for the Financial System', Speech delivered in Hong Kong, 15 September.

Gustke, Constance (2005) 'Going Around Banks', *CFO Magazine*, 15 October.

Hedge Fund Manager Week (2007) 'PE and HFs Join Forces in US Buyout', *Hedge Fund Manager Week*, London, 17 February, pp. 3, 14–15.

Independent, The (2007) 'The Big Question: So What Is Private Equity, and Is It Helpful or Damaging to the Economy?', 27 February.

Kuhnen, Camelia M. (Northwestern University) and Zweibel, Jeffrey (Stanford University) (2007) *Executive Pay, Hidden Compensation and Managerial Entrenchment*, Working paper, 15 March.

Lerner, Josh and Schoar, Antoinette (2004) 'To BDC or Not to BDC: The Promise and Perils of "Public Private Equity"', *Private Equity Report* (New York, Debevoise & Plimpton), Summer, p. 22.

O'Sullivan, Kate (2006) 'Rising Stakes – How the Strength of Private Equity is Changing M&A for Corporate Buyers', *CFO Magazine*, 1 July.

Packer, Frank, Stever, Ryan and Upper, Christian (2007) 'The Covered Bond Market', *BIS Quarterly Review*, September, pp. 43–55.

Partnoy, Frank (2006) 'How and Why Credit Rating Agencies Are Not Like Other Gatekeepers', *Legal Studies Research Paper Series*, Research paper no. 07-46, University of San Diego, School of Law, May.

Plender, John (2006) 'Limits of Disclosure', *Financial Times*, 31 July, p. 18.

Saffayeh, George and Lotem, Guy (2005/6) 'A Marriage of Convenience: Private Equity and Hedge Funds', *Cross Currents,* Ernst & Young, Winter, pp. 15–17, 30.

Stuart, Alix (2008) 'Rating Agencies – Over-Rated?', *CFO Europe*, September, pp. 55–8.

Tillman, Vickie A. (2003) *Regulating Credit Rating Agencies*, Standard & Poor's, October.

Tomlinson, Richard and Evans, David (2007) 'The Ratings Charade', *Bloomberg* markets, July 2007, pp. 50–61 (also http:/www.bloomberg.com/news/marketsmag/ratings).

US House of Representatives, Committee on Oversight and Government Reform (2007) *Hearings on Executive Pay: The Role of Compensation Consultants*, 5 December.

Wagner, Stephen and Dittmar, Lee (2006) 'The Unexpected Benefits of Sarbanes–Oxley', *Harvard Business Review,* Boston, Mass., April, pp. 133–40.

Weir, Helen, Lloyds TSB Finance Chief (2006) Interview, *Guardian,* 31 July, p. 20.

Westphal, James (University of Michigan) and Clement, Michael (University of Texas) (2007) 'Socio-political Dynamics in Relations between Top Managers and Security Analysts', Academy of Management Annual Meeting, Philadelphia, August.

5
Business Leaders, Stakeholders and the Value Pie – A Summing-up

It is difficult to encapsulate the principal qualities of business leadership. Nevertheless, several analysts have focused on the essential quality of creating lasting value and apportioning it among all stakeholders in a balanced way, i.e. commensurate with the effective contribution of each party. The foregoing quality of leadership is deemed vital to the cohesion of the enterprise and is a crucial catalyst susceptible of triggering the energies of all stakeholders to enlarge further their enterprise's value pie. This chapter attempts to sum up main issues and challenges in this area, including the issue of gauging the effective contribution-cum-compensation of various stakeholders in the process of value creation.

Success profiles

Exhibit 5.1 proposes a desirable profile for a business leader in the PE sector. However, the multiple characteristics presented below are seldom found in a single person – no matter how accomplished s/he is. A successful PE firm is typically led by a few entrepreneurial *partners*, bound by mutual trust and interests, and supported by a team with the requisite *talents*, *skills* and *experience*. The team is not a mere agglomeration of expertise; they need to 'dovetail' their efforts to produce – through effective synergy – the sought-after results. Partners, with their associates and teams of experts, acting as a coherent group, generally reach more *balanced* evaluations and decisions compared to a single individual.

Exhibit 5.1 A PE leader's traits of success

1. *Entrepreneurial* – endowed with: vision and strategy, business acumen, wise judgement, nerve for the timely seizure of opportunities (with respect to mobilizing and investing capital resources), strategic direction of promising 'investee companies' to create substantial net value before ultimate disinvestment, and capacity to build an optimal portfolio – all underpinned by risking his/her own money in the PE investment vehicle.
2. *Team builder* – with the capacity to (a) select, attract and guide diverse talented individuals with complementary skills, and 'mould' their efforts into serving the same objectives; (b) motivate, inspire, delegate, communicate and retain talented personnel for the right jobs in a trusting, synergetic work environment; (c) partner with appropriate parties; and (d) readily solve problems as they arise.
3. *Managerial-technical skills* – polyvalent: abreast and retentive of the latest developments in accounting, finance, economics, judicial and fiscal matters, organization, reporting, and industrial management; attuned to changing trends and early warning systems.
4. *Pro-active* – astute and convincing negotiator, insatiable curiosity allied to a critical mind, sociable, a communicator, persuasive, collegial, perspicacious, versatile, diplomatic, patient, empathic, reliable, readily responsive to client needs, and capable of working with flexibility and under pressure.
5. *Deal-making aptitude* – proven capacity at mastering complex situations to conclude timely business acquisitions or disinvestments; a thorough understanding of targeted companies – with respect to management's quality, products, costs, customers, competition, prospects and problems, among others.
6. *Experienced* – capitalizing on his/her network of business relationships; continuous capacity to make good use of past successes and/or failures.

Note: On the significance of characteristics and abilities of private equity CEOs, see, for example: Kaplan *et al.*, 2007; see also *The Economist*, 2006; and Groysberg *et al.*, 2006.

Top management of PE firms can be evaluated by reference to their mastering the multiple functions of the PE process. This covers the successful closing of promising and/or complex private equity deals (after the requisite investigations) and nurturing acquired companies to increase significantly their value up to the moment of disinvestment.

The successful acquisition of companies in foreign countries generally requires from one or more key individuals in the PE team proficiency in the language of the countries concerned, a profound understanding and respect for their cultures and customs, and personal experience in their companies in order to strengthen bonds of trust. Using local talent in such acquisitions contributes to operational effectiveness (see Brett *et al.*, 2006; and Eddy *et al.*, 2006).

The 'team' model has a relatively flat hierarchical structure which facilitates communication, brainstorming, consulting and sharing in the decision-making process. The PE team with the characteristics presented above normally carries out a careful and exhaustive SWOT (strengths, weaknesses, opportunities and threats) analysis of targeted companies. A variety of factors have to be identified and evaluated, at both the macro and micro levels. These include, in particular, the market position of the targeted company and its insulation from competitors; uniqueness of its products; scope for further development and prospects for innovation; customer and supplier diversification; modernity of the tools of production; critical mass; quality of the personnel (skills, age structure, continuity of training, loyalty, synergy and so on); management's efficiency and rapid responsiveness to customers needs; efficient reporting system; cost control and growth potential (see also Dobbs, 2006).

The definitive evaluation of an investment or a portfolio of investments – and, by implication, of the executives responsible for these investments – is made retrospectively when investments are wound up. An investment (or a portfolio of investments) can thus be judged to be of superior performance only when the ultimate exit produces a higher return compared with the average yield of investments in the same category of risks. One cannot neglect the role of luck. Expressed differently, *windfalls* may occasionally befall a party, and may not be linked to any particular effort, skill or creativity factors provided by the benefiting party. They may be a result of extraneous factors that create *excess* profits over given time periods – such as

(a) situations of dominant positions or restrictions of trade that are unchallenged or condoned by the regulatory authorities; and/or (b) booming general business conditions.

A PE firm naturally has to have a strategy of grooming junior executives for leadership, to succeed retiring PE leaders. Beyond technical skills, the junior executives' mantle for leadership has to be tested and proven – by reference to their concrete accomplishments. The succession process is a strategic requirement for a PE firm if it is to preserve its reputation among both investors and investee companies (actual and potential), and to enhance its value over the long term (see Jeanneret, 2006).

Revenues and compensations

Revenues

A PE firm – which services one or more PE funds (and possibly other pools of investments) – derives its income from a variety of functions relating to setting up, managing and winding up these funds. Typically, its income consists of (a) a fund-raising fee (1.5 per cent on committed capital); (b) a management fee (of 1.5 per cent to 2 per cent of the value of assets under management, including investors' money even if it is not put to work); *plus* (c) an incentive known as *carry* (generally 20 per cent) of net capital gains above an agreed *hurdle rate* (of 6 per cent to 10 per cent payable to investors) often linked to the prevailing cost of capital. The fee figures mentioned above are influenced, *inter alia*, by the quality of PE management and by the intensity of competition in the sector (see, for example, House of Commons, 2007). Fees cover in particular multiple categories of services already presented in Chapter 3 (see Exhibit 3.1).

Some of the previously mentioned functions can be farmed out to investment bankers or to specialist firms (such as M&A boutiques, tax advisers, accountants/auditors, lawyers, custodians and others). Fees payable to these entitites or individuals are usually expressed in (a) absolute terms based on the number of experts involved, and the time span of their involvement in the services offered; they reflect the importance and complexity of the services provided by the mandated party(ies), as well as the risks – if any – assumed by these parties; and (b) in relative terms to the size of capital pledged by investors or assets under management. Built-in incentives in the fee structure motivate investment bankers and other service providers to seek the best possible performance in satisfying the objectives of their clients (the buyers or sellers of companies or assets).

Fees and 'carry' received by PE firms can cumulatively be substantial. The management fee is usually calculated on the basis of the size of assets under management, regardless of the performance of these assets. Investors legitimately query the propriety of such fixity – especially when these funds are under-performing by reference to the S&P (Standard & Poor's) benchmark or other indices of publicly traded shares. Moreover, investors criticize such payments when no returns are generated, and prefer to disburse committed funds when acquisitions are finally made. Performance-related fees plus 'carry' payable to the GP (PE fund's management) is the guiding principle that the LP (investors) generally prefer.

In comparison to fees, *carry* represents, in general, the potentially most important source of income for the management team of a PE fund. It consists essentially of capital gains that are generated upon the sale of investments. Key executives in the management team of a PE fund are thus prompted to provide their very best efforts in: sourcing deals, structuring and managing investments, and working long enough with the PE fund in order to cash in the expected 'carry' benefits. The PE team is likely to develop a proclivity for limiting the nurturing period of investee companies, in order to cash in their 'carry' in potential capital gains in the shortest possible time. Such a proclivity could prompt PE management, in some cases, to raise financial returns from investee companies by slashing payrolls or reducing capital expenditure on research and development to show attractive current returns at the stated exit date (see Exhibit 2.1 in Chapter 2).

In venture capital, preferred investors can require 'liquidation preferences' in the form of a guaranteed return on their investment before any one else receives payment. This guarantee relegates the remaining shareholders in the investee company to a subordinate position (see Blaydon and Horvath, 2002).

Material compensations

For an enterprise's management, a crucial *motivation* in creating value is their expected share in the benefits they help to generate.

Incentive-based compensation can promote entrepreneurship, innovation, efficient management and synergy among stakeholders. To enable decision-makers to reach that situation, they need *optimal* arrangements for the splitting of profits – capable of yielding a high degree of satisfaction among key stakeholders, leading to a united and unfaltering drive in achieving set goals. Such arrangements can be a significant source of growth, particularly if compensation packages are not overly focused on the short term at the expense of a superior long-term performance.

It is generally agreed that human beings are driven to perform if they are adequately motivated by the expectation of appropriate personal rewards. Investors (referred to commonly as the *principal*) and their mandated managers (acting as their *agent*) compete to increase the size of their respective slices in the 'value creation pie' of an enterprise (see, for example, Kaplan and Strömberg, 2001). To avoid situations in which managers attempt to increase their power or personal benefits at the expense of investors or shareholders (known as the 'agency gap' conundrum), incentive schemes seek to align managers' compensation to shareholders' return.

Instead of limiting PE gains to investors and top management, statesmen and decision-makers have advocated the advantages of letting employees share in these gains. Thus, Jacques Chirac (when he was president of the French Republic) proposed on 3 January 2007 – but his proposal was not acted upon through legislation – that 20 per cent of a PE fund's capital gain should to be allocated to employees (see *L'Usine Nouvelle*, Paris, 11 January 2007, p. 62). A French senator and major industrialist, Serge Dassault, stated that his enterprise had allocated a portion of profits to employees for more than twenty years, thereby sparing his enterprise debilitating strikes and motivating all the parties concerned to create wealth (Session of the French Senate of 26 October 2008; for full official transcript, see: www.senat.fr). A leader of a major PE fund in France (Dominique Senequier, chairman and CEO of AXA Private Equity, with over US$22 billion under management in 2008) called for a mandatory legal distribution to all the employees of 5 per cent of the capital gain generated from the sale of any PE fund. In the absence of such a law, Ms Senequier urges European PE firms to draw up a voluntary code of conduct for splitting capital gains among investors, managers and employees, a proposal that has apparently encountered resistance from other PE groups (see *The Economist*, 2008; *Financial Times*, 13 July 2008, available at: FT.com).

Compensation packages containing profit participation formulae are generally intended as a driving force of motivation for managers and employees (regardless of gender or cultural background), to stimulate them in the wealth creation process for the enterprise. The problem is to define performances and benefits objectively, and to ascertain the actual contribution of executives and employees concerned.

Managers' *material* rewards cover a motley range of benefits, notably: bonuses, profit-sharing arrangements and 'carry' that can be exercised after set periods, notably after disinvestment. Other benefits received by privileged executives would comprise housing and recreational facilities, family allowances, insurances (health/dental/vision/accident and others), severance pay, extended paid holidays, loan forgiveness, employer-sponsored seminars, company-provided transport, products/ services gratuity or discounts, country-club membership, and various other fringe benefits and perks.

Official investigations (parliamentary, judicial and administrative), researchers and the media have brought to the general public's attention the ostentatious cupidity of certain top executives. The pay packages of a few of these executives have been deemed to be *excessive* – with no relationship to their contribution to *value creation* in the enterprise and/or to *personal hardships* (physical, mental, psychic or moral) they might have encountered while carrying out their professional duties. Indeed, cases exist of large compensation/retirement packages obtained by self-serving executives who have performed poorly (or even negatively) in the businesses they were entrusted to manage (see, for example, *Financial Times*, 2006, and *The Economist*, 2007).

Public policy and corporate governance have to guard against allowing a culture of *greed* and *selfish short-term interest* to develop, as expressed by a US veteran leader of financial groups (Vojta, 2009). Performance objectives that favour excessive risk-taking with other people's funds could well lead to losses, and possibly fraud or other violations. This calls for holding executives effectively accountable to their performance in serving the firm's goals and priorities (see, for example, Leslie *et al.*, 2006). When generous compensation packages are offered to CEOs and other top executives to entice them to perform, it is legitimate for owners of businesses to require 'claw back' clauses; executives will then return a portion of their past or current pay packages if their performances fail to attain agreed benchmarks during their tenure.

Non-material incentives

The behaviour of human beings is driven by multiple forces, and influenced by a variety of factors. With respect specifically to the process of value creation, several parties have highlighted humans' motivation in the *maximization of their personal monetary/material gain,* with little or no concern regarding impact on others – whether positive, neutral or negative. Nevertheless, one should acknowledge the existence of other motives which complement, boost or constrain the foregoing motive of 'filthy lucre'. Among these, one can mention the socio-ethical ones that prompt individuals to superior performance in their quest to excel – not only for their exclusive benefit, but also for the benefit of others (see cases in Chapter 1). Rewards can thus be a mix of material (generally measurable in financial terms) and non-material (improved self-image, moral satisfaction, social recognition, political influence or spiritual fulfilment).

It is possible for investors to obtain attractive returns over the long term, if they invest in firms that observe socio-ethical principles in their business activities. Guidelines for such investments generally cover, as well as the professional responsibility of continuous improvement in performance, the following principles: (a) the fair treatment and protection of the rights of all stakeholders (workers, customers, creditors/investors, partners, subcontractors, local communities and others) in addition to the rights of owners and management; (b) transparent and honest operations; and (c) good corporate citizenship through respect for the legal, social and natural environment (see, for example, www.domini.com; www.cdcgroup.com; also The Declaration of Bern, *Responsible Money: How to Invest in an Ethical, Ecological and Social Manner*, February 2008; available at: www.ladb.ch).

Chief among the non-material rewards is *pride* or *love* for one's own work. These sentiments derive from such factors as empowerment, enhanced reputation, social/ethical recognition, healthy work environment, balanced work/leisure time, job stability and security, a sense of 'fair treatment' – to mention just a few. Non-material rewards can, in a number of situations, prove to be significant in harnessing the energies of management and personnel, and in mobilizing or sustaining their creativity or ardour.

Business leaders and their employees can thus be driven by multiple legitimate motives: personal material gain as well as social, ethical or civic motives (see Box 5.1). Among high net worth business leaders, one could mention a few widely reported by the media (notably Warren Buffett and Bill Gates) at the beginning of the twenty-first century, who offered $US multi-billion-dollar donations to charity. These people have been motivated in their business creativity by the dual objectives of (a) accumulating sizeable personal wealth; and (b) allocating a substantial portion of that wealth to philanthropic missions, either during their lifetime or bequeathed in their wills. Such motives exist among a large number of other people of lesser wealth, though the smaller sums they contribute to society do not invite media attention.

Sharing gains among stakeholders: an elusive equilibrium?

The performance of an enterprise, as measured by benefits accruing to *all* of its stakeholders, is gaining in general acceptance. Authors of modern organizational theory advocate that the *raison d'être* of businesses is to create wealth for all their stakeholders. This has been clearly conveyed thus 'The conventional notion that the corporation should create wealth for its shareowners is incorrect. The corporation should be redefined to emphasize its relationships with and responsibilities toward *all* stakeholders, both voluntary and involuntary... The stakeholder model of the corporation fits in with broadly accepted normative and ethical considerations' (Post *et al.*, 2002).

The UNCTAD Intergovernmental Working Group of Experts, ISAR (International Standard of Accounting and Reporting, established by a resolution of the Economic and Social Council of the United Nations in October 1982) has identified a core set of indicators of stakeholders' business performance and a reporting methodology for each indicator. These business indicators are gradually coming into use among enterprises belonging to developed economies (where information is readily available) and increasingly in emerging economies (see United Nations: UNCTAD, 2008).

Box 5.1 Is philanthropy a source of business motivation?

A few entrepreneurs and managers can be more motivated if their business generates wealth not only for themselves and their shareholders or investors, but also for the benefit of other stakeholders and for marginalized members of society – with no relation to their business activities. This is the case of a manager of a hedge fund, Christopher Hohn, who pointedly named his fund 'The Children Investment Fund – TCI' after his charity 'The Children Investment Fund Foundation – CIFF' run by his wife, Jamie Cooper-Hohn. The Fund pays the Foundation 0.5 per cent of its assets annually, with another 0.5 per cent of assets annually if the Fund achieves returns in excess of 11 per cent.

CIFF is primarily concerned with alleviating child poverty in the developing world. It focuses on emergency humanitarian assistance, education, and the fight against HIV and AIDS – mainly in Africa and Asia. Mrs Cooper-Hohn said that 'the foundation is Chris's motivation to work hard and get the returns' for investors – subject to funnelling a pre-determined portion to CIFF.

Investors had to accept the *formulaic permanent link* between the assets of TCI and the annual contributions to TCI's charitable arm, CIFF, established in 2003 – as a key factor of motivating Mr Hohn to super-perform. The TCI hedge fund had assets estimated at more than £5 billion in 2008.

Mr Hohn, the son of a car mechanic, also made sizeable *ad hoc* contributions out of his personal income, earned thanks to his talent and skills in the management of investors' money. Donations by Mr Hohn and TCI to CIFF had exceeded £800 million by mid-2008.

Most of TCI's investors have reportedly been *neutral* about the above-mentioned formulaic pre-condition, so long as the fund manager produced for them particularly attractive returns, which he has done. Some of his institutional or high net worth investors have, one should add, their own charity vehicles.

Sources: 'The Couple behind the £466m Charity Donation', 24 June 2008; available at: www.telegraph.co.uk; also 'Interview with Jamie Cooper-Hohn', *Sunday Telegraph*, London, 22 June 2008'; 'Interview with Christopher Hohn, *Institutional Investor Magazine*, New York, 12 April 2007; James Mackintosh, 'Hohn Follows Bumper Years at TCI with Massive Donation', 21 June 2008 – available at: FT.com.

Business leaders have therefore multiple objectives for the performance of their enterprises. For those concerned with the long-term prosperity of their business in competitive markets, core objectives cover: (a) the expansion of their enterprise's 'value-added pie'; (b) alignment of stakeholders' motivation in the 'wealth generation process' in order to obtain efficiency gains and increases in profits; and (c) a balanced and fair split of net wealth generated for the benefit of all contributing stakeholders, thereby averting potential conflicts or crises. Time horizons to attain objectives are likely to be longer for breakthrough technological innovations (see Case A in Chapter 1) compared to financial services and artisanal/artistic works (Cases B and C, also in Chapter 1).

Splitting the 'value-added pie' of a business among top and middle management, employees, investors and other stakeholders (listed in Exhibit 5.2) is often the outcome of relative bargaining powers. Some empirical research suggests that institutional investors in PE funds (notably pension funds) have not obtained average yields superior to those of traded securities (as measured by the S&P 500 index), in view of the hefty cuts in gains going to PE partners and executives (Kaplan and Schoar, 2005; and Phalippou and Gottschalg, 2007).

Managers of a PE fund are generally more incentive-driven should a significant portion of their personal wealth be invested in the fund. This would encourage them to be particularly prudent, especially when faced with appropriate *claw-back* clauses. The latter require maintaining the realization of benefits contingent on the proven performance of decision-making managers, as judged over a reasonably long period (notably the holding period of the portfolio of acquisitions or investments).

Performance-linked benefits – modulated in relation to the functions and responsibility of the manager concerned – should prompt

Exhibit 5.2 Stakeholders vying for the 'value pie': a classification

1 Executive owners/partners, managers, and employees.
2 Investors and other financiers.
3 Suppliers, subcontractors and other business partners.
4 Service providers: investment advisers, lawyers, accountants, consultants and others.
5 Customers.
6 Community members and concerned civil society groups.
7 Public authorities (interested in fiscal revenues, job creation, know-how transfer, trade and other public interest benefits).

Note: See also United Nations: UNCTAD, 2008, p. 6.

him/her to exercise continuous high vigilance to avoid blunders or *excessive* risk-taking (see, for example, Rajan, 2005). In fact, the ill-considered and risky actions of a few executives have resulted in multi-billion-dollar losses for investors/lenders. Occasionally, such executives retired from their institutions with 'golden' parachutes, regardless of their negative performances or the debacles for which they were responsible. These executives were then free to start other activities with equanimity (see, for example, Thomas 2008; available at: nytimes.com).

For a judicious approach, one could recommend that PE executives' payable incentive benefits (in cash, equity rights or other forms), over and above regular salaries, could be put in escrow accounts – to be released upon the winding-up of the PE fund. The size of these benefits should be based on the ultimate net performance of PE investments. The great difficulty of calibrating 'compensation packages' relates to the 'real performance' of each member of the management team and their collaborators, judged over the long term; such judgement must beware of 'opportunistic grabbing' or 'free riding'. The optimum split of benefits between investors, managers and other stakeholders have to be reviewed and refined – as warranted – to sustain *wealth creation*, and minimize *conflict* or *stress*. Indeed, the critical challenge is to calibrate properly compensation packages of the PE team to avoid dissensions that would sap the drive for value creation. Moreover, incentives for managers should not be at the expense of other stakeholders and the prosperity of investee companies.

Tales of human fallibility continue to occur, along with ingenious fraudulent ways being found to circumvent regulations – whether in developed or developing economies. Determined and ingenious people – often tempted by greed or unethical motives – are likely to outsmart rules and circumvent controls, and could well elude detection by security systems, especially when operational risks are evident from combining the duties of transaction, recording and control under the aegis of one person. This can be illustrated eloquently by Bernard L. Madoff's 'Ponzi scheme' swindle of some US$65 billion, which came to light in December 2008 (see testimonies presented on 5 January 2009 at the US House Committee on Financial Services on *Assessing the Madoff Ponzi and the Need for Regulatory Reform*, chaired by Congressman Paul E. Kanjorski; available at: www.house.gov; and 27 January 2009 at US Senate Committee on Banking, Housing, and Urban Affairs, *Madoff Investment Securities Fraud: Regulatory and Oversight Concerns and the Need for Reform*, chaired by Senator Christopher J. Dodd; available at: www.senate.gov).

The hypothesis that PE funds provide superior means (compared to other financial intermediaries) of dynamizing entrepreneurship for the benefit of all stakeholders and for society at large is unconfirmed. Comprehensive studies conducted recently (covering 21,397 private equity transactions between 1970 and 2007) did not produce definitive results on key issues affecting PE stakeholders. Further rigorous analyses based on complete, comparable, up-to-date and authentic data are needed to evaluate the impact of the 'private equity' sector on *key economic variables*, analysed in different environments and markets. Variables include notably job creation, turnover, efficiency, innovation, net value creation, governance, economic growth and social progress, among others (see Lerner and Gurung, 2008; available at: www.weforum.org). Such information is lacking since PE firms are not subject to mandatory regulations that obligate them to issue regular transparent reports (similar to those obtaining for publicly listed companies). They are generally loath to disclose information voluntarily, as they deem this to be 'proprietary'.

References

Blaydon, Colin and Horvath, Michael (2002) 'Liquidation Preferences: What You May Not Know', *Venture Capital Journal*, March.

Brett, J., Behfar, K., and Kern, M. (2006) 'Managing Multicultural Teams', *Harvard Business Review*, November, pp. 84–91.

Dobbs, Richard (2006) 'Creating Value from Mergers', *The McKinsey Quarterly*, no. 4, pp. 4–5.

Economist, The (2006) 'A Survey of Talent – The Battle for Brainpower', 7 October.

Economist, The (2007) 'In the Money – A Special Report on Executive Pay', 20 January.

Economist, The (2008) 'Buy Out and Pay Up', 26 July p. 69.

Eddy, James, Hall, Stephen J. D. and Robinson, Stephen R. (2006) 'How Global Organizations Develop Local Talent', *The McKinsey Quarterly*, no. 3, pp. 6–8.

Financial Times (2006) 'Gilded Age: How a Corporate Elite Is Leaving Middle America Behind', 21 December, p. 11.

Groysberg, Boris, McLean, Andrew N. and Nohria, Nitin (2006) 'Are Leaders Portable?', *Harvard Business Review*, May, pp. 92–100.

House of Commons (2007) *Private Equity, Tenth Report of Session 2006–07*, (London: The Stationery Office Limited), 30 July.

Jeanneret, Richard (2006) 'PE Succession Planning: Don't Put It Off', *Cross Currents*, Ernst & Young, Summer, pp. 20–3.

Kaplan, Steven N., Klebanov, Mark M. and Sorensen, Morten (2007) 'Which CEO Characteristics and Abilities Matter?', Working paper, University of Chicago Graduate School of Business, June.

Kaplan, Steven N. and Schoar, Antoinette (2005) 'Private Equity Performance: Returns, Persistence and Capital Flows', *The Journal of Finance*, pp. 1791–1823.

Kaplan, Steven N. and Strömberg, Per (2001) 'Venture Capitalists as Principals: Contracting, Screening, and Monitoring', *AEA Papers and Proceedings*, vol. 91, no. 2, May, pp. 426–30.

Lerner, Josh (Harvard Business School) and Gurung, Anuradha (World Economic Forum) (2008) *The Global Economic Impact of Private Equity Report 2008* (Switzerland: World Economic Forum).

Leslie, Keith, Loch, Mark A. and Schaninger, William (2006) 'Managing Your Organization by the Evidence', *The McKinsey Quarterly*, no. 3, pp. 65–75.

Phalippou, Ludovic (University of Amsterdam) and Gottschalg, Oliver (HEC Paris) (2007) *Performance of Private Equity Funds*, Working paper, Social Science Research Network, May.

Post, James E., Preston, Lee E. and Sachs, Sybille (2002) *Redifining the Corporation, Stakeholder Management and Organizational Wealth*, pp. 32–3.

Rajan, Raghuram (2005) 'Straight Talk – Risky Business', *Finance and Development* (Washington, DC: International Monetary Fund), September, pp. 54–6.

Thomas, Landon, Jr. (2008) 'What's $34 Billion on Wall Street?', *The New York Times*, 27 January.

United Nations: UNCTAD (2008) *Guidance on Corporate Responsibility Indicators in Annual Reports*, Geneva.

Vojta, George J. (2009) 'Private Sector Corruption Justifies Society's Clawback Demand', *The RMA Journal*, The Risk Management Association, April, pp. 23–25.

Part 3
Investment Dynamics

From his vantage position of expertise and rich experience in the intertwined fields of finance and entrepreneurship, Professor Benoit Leleux offers in chapter 6 an original contribution on private equity's role within the financial system. His analysis employs a broad holistic approach, judiciously cutting across periods of growth or recession. Professor Leleux's findings present eloquently – for the benefit of professionals, policy makers and academics – the fundamental dynamic forces affecting private equity's role in wealth creation over the long term.

The book concludes with a succinct reflection on a propitious environment for progress.

6
Private Equity as a Wealth Recycler

Benoit Leleux
Stephan Schmidheiny Professor of Entrepreneurship and Finance, IMD (International Institute for Management Development), Lausanne, Switzerland

The great capitalistic washing machine

Rooted at the heart of capitalism is the belief that the system, with all its flaws and inbuilt inequalities, remains the most efficient asset allocator; that is, that it is best able to channel scarce resources (money, capital and technologies) into their most efficient uses. In other words, while it may be difficult to support it philosophically or ethically, a capitalistic economic system proves its worth every day in its ability to generate the largest amount of wealth. Ethics and philosophy can then be employed to determine how best to allocate the created wealth.

But how is this great wealth engine functioning? What oils the system and makes it rev at high speeds without any destructive friction? How do certain variations in the capitalistic system work better than others; generating more jobs and creating more wealth than others? What I suggest here is that private equity (used in its broadest sense to cover all forms of 'private' capital, such as venture capital, buyouts, restructuring, mezzanine and so on), in its capacity to recycle long-term capital towards the most dynamic segments of the economy, is the ultimate turbocharger of a capitalistic economy, providing not only the fuel to enable it to grow faster but also the power to discipline actors and the oil to smooth the capital market's short-term vagaries. In other words, I argue that private equity is not only necessary but in fact indispensable to the proper functioning of a capitalistic system. I review these arguments in a later part of the chapter, in light of the credit crunch and global economic crisis of 2007–8 and offer scenarios for the future of private equity.

The long-term capital virtuous circle

The simplest possible way to describe what we refer to implicitly as the greatest wealth recycler is to consider a long-term capital perspective of the world. This is done graphically in Exhibit 6.1.

Let us start at the bottom of the exhibit, with Growth and job creation. What is 'wealth' at a macroeconomic level? Practically speaking, it is a combination of high employment levels and the capacity to create value; that is, national production (gross domestic product (GDP), gross national product (GNP) and so on). For this to happen, firms, and in particular the most dynamic ones, must (i) have access to sufficient long-term capital; and (ii) be submitted to sufficiently stringent scrutiny and discipline to be continuously driven to 'deliver' results. The second element in this equation is the one that is often missing in the traditional economic recipe. Just as the notion of the 'new individual', disinterested and supportive of the common good, flawed the communist ideology irremediably, so has the capitalistic one been all too willing to subscribe to the notion of firms being subject to self-discipline and control. The reality is that

Exhibit 6.1 The private equity wealth recycler

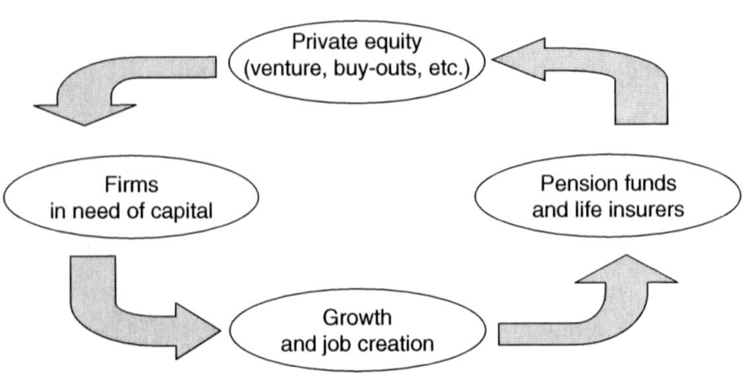

the current systems of governance are mainly very weak. Internally, boards of directors and other control mechanisms do not have the means (human resources, independence, access to funds) to collect information and intervene if needed. Externally, capital markets and public shareholders do not have the incentives to act on behalf of others because of a free-riding problem. So, in the atomistic world of public ownership with weak internal governance, who will in effect discipline firms and lead them to the greatest wealth creation?

Private equity is the ultimate embodiment of private wealth. It has largely been subject to limited reporting, control and taxation. In a sense, and without an official endorsement by governments, private equity has been treated in a 'special' way. Historically, some of that treatment was in recognition of the critical importance of such players in the proper functioning of the economy.

Venture capitalists (to include in this case both formal investors, such as venture capital funds, and informal investors, mainly high net worth individuals or 'angels') were willing to put their capital at risk and provide support to emerging new ventures, where very few other financial actors would have been willing or able to provide support. These new ventures are the innovators, the model breakers, the breakthrough thinkers of the economy. By definition, they are rare and small at the beginning, but they carry the potential to create or radically redefine whole industries. They are the long-term catalysts for change and growth, the 'money of invention', as described by Gompers and Lerner (2001).

Buy-out funds are the catalysts for a different kind of change: one that affects more established firms. A well-known failing of human nature is that success breeds contempt and arrogance. Every firm, at one time or another, falls prey to self-satisfaction, less-than-optimal management, is simply not able to gather sufficient means to pursue aggressive – that is, more risky – development strategies, or requires massive restructuring that is unfathomable to the current owners. Buy-out capital provides the means to rejuvenate growth, to kick-start a new cycle of development. It is the 'money of growth' in a sense, the one that provides established firms with the means or the incentive to start looking again at new ways to expand.

Up to now, we have looked only at private equity as a source of capital for firms. The 'missing link' that ties the system together and provides the turbocharger to make the economic engine rev to super performance levels is the right-hand component of Exhibit 6.1 – the long-term sources of capital embodied mainly in life insurance and pension funds. (In the USA, it would also be key to discuss the role played by university endowments in that system. These are also very long-term capital sources, with limited constraints and high return needs. They constitute a prime source of inflows into the private equity industry there.) What both life insurance and pension funds share is a very long-term perspective, with liabilities (in case of death or retirement) that can be determined relatively precisely forty or fifty years in advance, as well as a need to generate sufficient revenues from the funds invested to cover those liabilities when they are due. These long-term, motivated and patient investors are the fuel of the system: without their inflows, the engine grinds to a halt.

Private equity and wealth creation

Measuring the actual economic impact of buy-out and venture capital is no easy task. In particular, it is impossible to compare scenarios, or use a traditional placebo research design. Firms that do benefit from private equity injections and the subsequent supervision and guidance are not a random sample of firms drawn from the population at large but a carefully selected subsample with unique characteristics. All this leads to a situation where measuring wealth creation is a very arduous task. The evidence, despite the methodological shortcomings, is relatively strong to support clear economic benefits to the intervention of private equity investors. One of the most often quoted studies in Europe is the one conducted by EVCA (European Venture Capital and Private Equity Association, the trade group representing European private equity investors) in 2000. It looked at a sample of companies across Europe that had undergone a private, equity-backed buyout between 1992 and 1997. With over 300 responses, it highlighted the fact that more than 84 per cent of responding companies stated unequivocally that, without the buy-out, they would either have ceased to trade or have grown less strongly. The vast majority of respondents acknowledged that the contribution of the private equity investors – in both financial and non-financial aspects of company operations – has been crucial to post-buy-out success. The economic and social impact of the buy-out on investee companies could be seen in virtually every one of a wide variety of indicators – from increased sales and profits, higher levels of employment and employee earnings, through to a larger percentage of exports, better marketing and improved customer service. Two-thirds of respondents reported that they had outperformed their competitors over the five years 1992 to 1997.

Many other studies, in the USA and Europe, support a similar view: firms that have benefited from buy-out and venture capital tend to outperform their peers in terms of growth, employment creation, and other financial and non-financial measurements. The question remains, of course, as to whether these firms would have outperformed their peers *without* the interventions; that is, whether private equity investors are simply good at spotting existing growth and value creation opportunities, or if they in fact set the stage and actively create them.

An interesting alternative approach was used by Sudarsanam *et al.* (2007). Using a sample of 236 UK companies that went from public to private (PTP) company status between 1997 and 2005, and a control sample of similar firms not going private, they find that companies going private had a significantly higher default probability, fewer growth opportunities, lower stock market valuations, poorer operating performance and larger pre-PTP management holdings. Weak corporate governance factors increased the chances of going private. Upon the announcement of the going private transaction, their value jumped 15 per cent. Private equity firms sponsoring PTPs generated higher shareholder value gains when they acquired firms with poorer growth records, higher risks of bankruptcy and larger free cash flows. Again, the value creation benefits of private equity intervention in these difficult circumstances seemed to be supported.

Sand in the virtuous cycle

But many things can and do derail this great circle of long-term wealth creation. In this section, we quickly review some of the largest impediments to the normal functioning of the system.

Insufficient numbers of long-term investors

One of the largest providers of long-term capital are capitalization-based pension systems, such as the ones prevailing in the USA, the UK or Chile. These pension systems free up capital from individuals and firms for long-term investment. Getting returns is key to obtaining a satisfactory pension, so incentives are strong to deliver performance and channel the funds into the most dynamic aspects of the economy. Whether the system operates on a defined contributions or defined benefits basis, someone (the individuals and their wealth managers in the first case, the firms and their pension managers in the second) will be strongly incentivized to put the money to the best (that is, the most profitable) use in the economy.

This is not the situation that prevails in economies relying mainly on redistribution-based pension systems, where current pension contributions from workers are used to pay the pensions of current retirees. This system lives to some extent from hand to mouth, collecting money from some and giving it to others. This eliminates entirely from the economic system one of the largest pools of long-term capital, with the most dramatic and unplanned consequences. While these systems were often set up to provide 'social safety nets', they in effect destroy the very basis on which long-term sustainable benefits can be offered to the largest segment of the population, by undermining the funding of those firms that ultimately employ the individuals.

Risk myopia

Another significant blockage in the system comes from bureaucratic interpretation of the concept of risk. In financial terms, risk is simply volatility, or the inability to predict exactly what returns will be over a time period. The relevant question is, of course, what time period is relevant or appropriate. Assets that are volatile over the short term can prove to be very different over the long term. For example, publicly listed stocks tend to be quite volatile on a weekly basis, but if one takes a fifty-year perspective, they have delivered remarkably consistently. When pension funds are analysed, as indicated above, they face relatively well-defined long-term liabilities. Short-term volatility, while unpleasant, does not have to antagonize their long-term survival or their ability to cover their obligations. So, when well-intentioned regulators impose, for example, minimal annual returns on them, however low, they are effectively imposing short-term constraints on long-term investment vehicles, severely biasing their investment allocations towards low risk/low return instruments, such as government bonds.

Governance breakdowns

The whole system is premised on individual responsibility; that is, each and every actor in the chain is properly incentivized to supervise and control its investments. In recent years (since about 2007), growth around the world, and, in particular, BRIC countries (the emerging economies of Brazil, Russia, India and China), have generated incredible amounts of liquidity, which has then been delivered to wealth managers around the world. Money managers were punished rapidly for not 'putting the money to work', through lower fees and withdrawals of capital, so a shortage of investment opportunities offering satisfactory risk–return profiles did not prevent them from pushing more and more money on to private equity or absolute return funds. The consequences of these poor investments will be borne by the investors, not the money managers. Similarly, the growth in securitization of fixed income instruments has generated a whole new generation of bankers behaving as initiators more than risk evaluators and risk bearers. In this new form, bankers generate money through initiating fees, not managing the debt over the long term.

While securitization generates liquidity in the system, it also relies on the ultimate holders to control the evolution of risk in the positions. But those positions become more and more 'aggregated', and hence difficult to control individually. Aggregation does not control or eliminate risk: it only pools it. You can slice and dice the risk pool any way you want, in as many delicately defined tranches, but ultimately someone has to manage and bear the risk in the underlying securities and positions. Pooling just creates an illusion of security through diversification. As every risk manager knows, in case of a catastrophic failure in the system, correlations between asset returns tend to converge towards one, virtually eliminating the risk-reducing benefits of diversification.

Another noticeable failure in the system is the reliance on external rating agencies to provide risk assessment for many securities. However professional these agencies might be, they never bear the full brunt of the consequences of their improper assessments. In a sense, they are very much like risk consultants, providing advice and guidance but without any guarantee of success. This point seems to have been lost on many new institutional investors, who have been all too willing to accept rating agencies' assessments. Risk agencies do not manage risk, nor do they suffer the consequences of their poor assessments.

Private equity in the subprime whirlwind (Summer 2007)

In late 2006, the opportunities for big and easy profits in private equity were seen as waning, as the world had been awash in cheap money for several years. A number of key factors had been combining to create a fertile environment for private equity:

(i) a global economic growth period, with BRIC countries showing exceptional performance. Global GDP growth during the period 2000–7 averaged 4.4 per cent per annum;
(ii) a very tame inflationary environment and persistent low interest rates across the world. The global core consumer price index excluding hyperinflation countries averaged around 2 per cent in 2002, dropped to about 1.4 per cent in 2004, then crept back up to a rather stable and mild 2 per cent until June 2007 (J. P. Morgan Chase data, cited in Walker *et al.*, 2007). The global average central bank policy interest rates moved over the same period from around 3 per cent per annum in 2002 to 2.2 per cent in 2004, climbing back up to about 4.3 per cent by June 2007;
(iii) the superb historical performance of buy-out funds, in particular when compared to other asset classes, such as venture capital and other fixed income instruments (see Exhibits 6.2 and 6.3). Particularly striking has been the superior risk/return profile of buy-out funds in Europe, where they have systematically delivered better returns than their riskier venture capital counterparts; and
(iv) the availability of high leverage for deals, a pre-condition to any buyout. Exhibit 6.4 illustrates the global fundraising situation for private equity during the period.

In response to the returns they were generating, private equity funds became replete with massive amounts of new funds. With such easy

Exhibit 6.2 5-year rolling internal rate of return for US private equity funds (as of 31 December 2007)

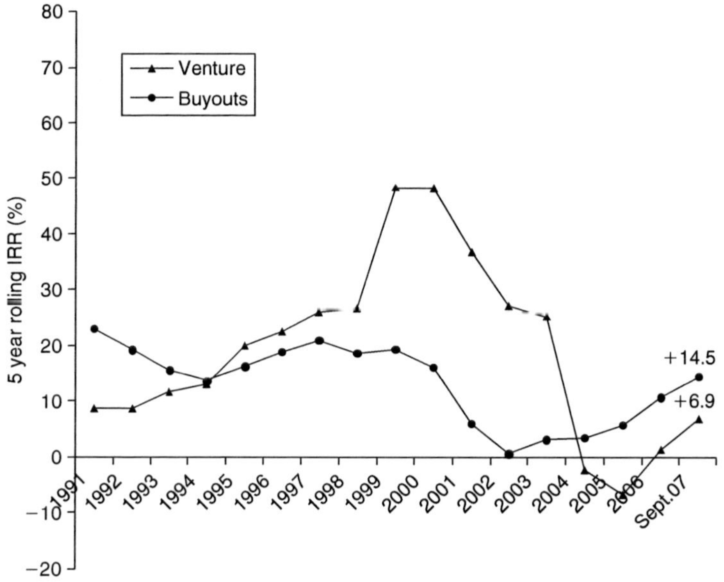

Source: Thomson Financial analysis for EVCA.

access to capital, the firms indulged in transaction sizes and quantities never seen before. Blackstone, for example, one of the largest funds in existence, announced deals in 2006 that were three times the size of those announced in 2005, and six times of those of 2004. Other players were not far behind, with global private equity deals announced topping some $US730 billion for 2006 alone, and 2007 already showing all the signs of easily beating that figure.

The party came to a crashing end with the sudden credit crunch generated by the subprime mortgage market upheavals in the USA that started in June 2007. Suddenly, it became very clear to lenders (and *ex post* to the rating agencies in charge of evaluating the risk exposure in many of these instruments) that exposures were greater

Exhibit 6.3 5-year rolling IRR for European private equity funds (as of 31 December 2007)

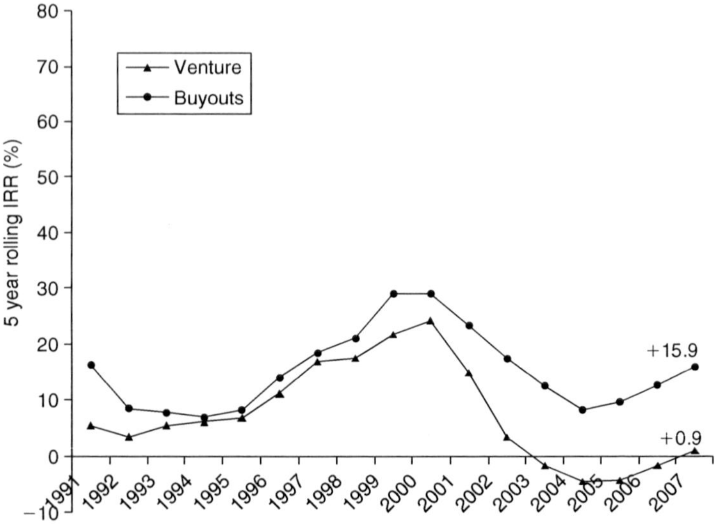

Source: Thomson Financial analysis for EVCA.

than they wished to believe, and hence that returns were totally inappropriate, leading to a re-pricing of many asset markets, starting, of course, with subprimes and their CMO (collateralized mortgage obligations, or securitized mortgages) brethren, but spreading quickly to other segments of the economy as many industry watchers pondered the depth of the affliction. As is always the case in such situations, it is the depth of the capital markets that suffered: the higher-risk segments of the commercial paper market very much shut down, thus depriving many actors from access to debt markets, at whatever cost (see Exhibit 6.5).

One sign that the PE markets were getting ahead of themselves was the trend in interest coverage ratios (cash flows divided by interest expenses) exhibited by private equity deals (see Exhibit 6.6). Despite the fact that money was flowing freely and real interest rates remained

Exhibit 6.4 Global fundraising situation for venture and buy-out funds, 2000–7

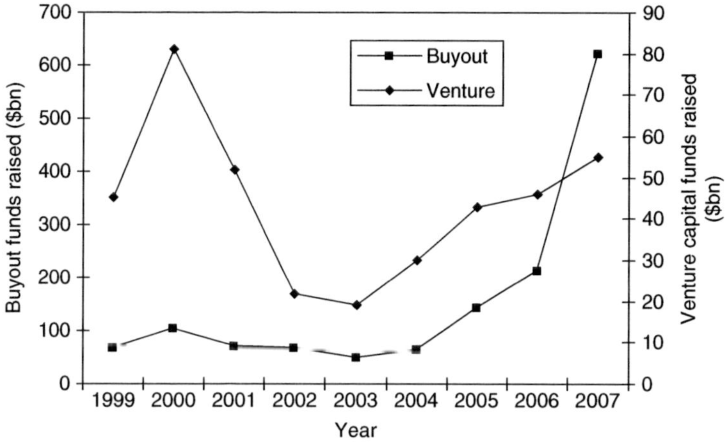

Sources: IFSL estimates based on PEREP Analytics, EVCA, Thomson Reuters/PwC, NVCA and Ernst & Young data.

Exhibit 6.5 Value of announced private equity buy-outs ($US billions)

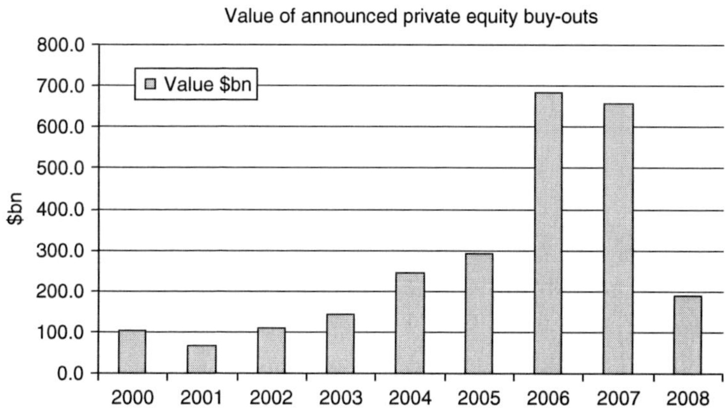

Source: Data provided by Dealogic, 19 February 2009.

Exhibit 6.6 Evolution of buy-out leverage over the period 1997–2007

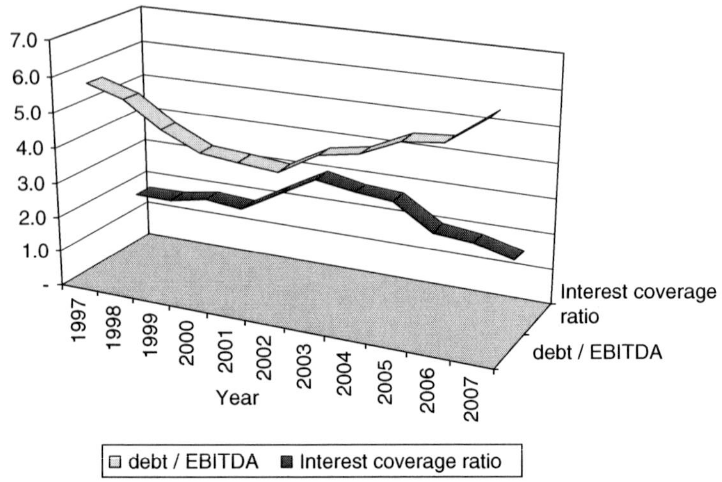

Source: S&P *Leveraged Buyout Review*, quoted in a Carlyle Group presentation.

close to historical lows in many currencies, the interest coverage ratios for gone private buy-outs, which were close to 1.7 in 1997, ran up to 3.5 in the 2000–4 tight credit markets, to dive again to around 1.5 by 2007. An interest coverage ratio of 1.5 meant that two-thirds of the annual cash flows of a company was being used to service debt, where a ratio of 3.5 meant less than 30 per cent of annual cash flow was being used towards debt-service, leaving more room for calamities.

Leverage multiples, expressed as the ratio of a firm's gross debt to current EBITDA(EBITDA = earnings before interest, taxes, depreciation and amortization; a common measure of operational profit), similarly crept up, from around ×4.0 in early 2002 to ×6.5 and above in 2007. In other words, firms were able to borrow up to 6.5 times their realized annual profits, levels that could only be justified if there was a belief in sustainably low interest rates and high economic growth (S&P Leveraged Commentary and Data in *Wall Street Journal Europe*, 14 June 2007).

Exhibit 6.7 Estimated sources of buy-out investment returns

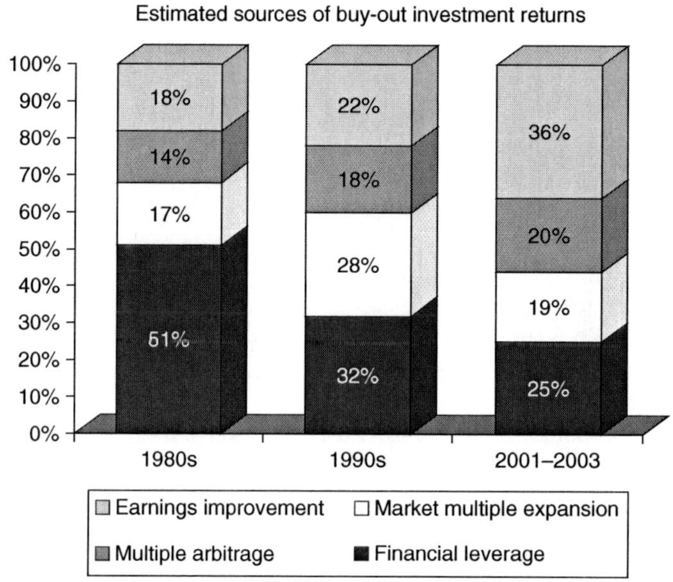

Historically, private equity investors earned their returns from the combination of four value creators:

- *Earnings improvements*, or the ability to generate fundamental profit improvements in the firms they acquired.
- *Multiple arbitrage*, also known as 'bottom feeding' or 'multiple surfing', obtained by buying companies at the bottom of their industry appeal (the trough of the down cycle) and selling them when they are back in fashion.
- *Market-multiple expansion*, or the ability to generate a better growth and profitability story behind the target company, hence supporting a great earnings multiple.
- *Financial leverage* or taking full advantage of the tax benefits of high leverage.

As shown in Exhibit 6.7, value creation in buy-outs evolved from a purely tax-driven leverage play into a mainly operational-driven play in the 1990s and the early years of the twenty-first century.

With firms in pretty good shape in mid-2007 (in part because of the disciplining power of a very active buy-out market, forcing firms to behave 'as if' under private equity ownership), with most industries at peaks of their cycles and with cheap leverage also very much history, the prospects for returns were indeed tame.

The 2008 credit crunch and beyond

The following year turned the 'cooling off' period of the private equity industry into the worst Siberian weather it had ever faced. All the factors that conspired to pump up the industry collapsed simultaneously. First, the debt bubble burst. From 2003 to 2007, annual debt issuance rocketed from US$71 billion to US$669 billion (Dealogic, December 9, 2008, cited in Meerkat and Liechtenstein, 2008). Banks found themselves nursing massive capital write-downs related to the subprime instruments, and many of them collapsed, including some famous Wall Street names such as Lehman Brothers. The bottom fell out of the market: issuances of LBO debt in the third quarter of 2008 were 75 per cent lower than in the comparable quarter of 2007. Second, a massive, global economic crisis struck, affecting growth and employment prospects. Company earnings dropped drastically, taking the stock markets down in their fall. Globally, stock prices fell by some 45 per cent in 2008, their worst performance ever recorded. Governments intervened, pumping unheard of amounts of money into economies, supporting banks and companies alike in a desperate attempt to restart growth. Unemployment spread rapidly, leading to deflation and cuts in interest rates. Third, and an indirect consequence of the above, many institutional investors were also licking their wounds from investments in private equity, reducing their allocations in the asset class altogether.

In the midst of this turmoil, private equity firms are faced with a conundrum. On the one hand, crisis and restructuring times usually breed fantastic opportunities. Companies are forced to restructure and rebalance their portfolios, selling non-core assets and other marginal entities. Furthermore, many funds sit on large amounts of uninvested commitments. An article in the *Wall Street Journal* in January

2009 suggested that the ten largest buy-out firms had around US$200 billion available to invest in buyouts. Some firms also tried to have their cake and eat it, buying back from bankers their own portfolio company debts at a discount, taking advantage of the even worse shape of some buy-out lenders (Mawson, 2009).

On the other hand, many resist the temptation to do deals so far because of continuing problems in the debt markets, uncertainty over the depth of the economic downturn and its impact on their portfolio companies, and problems with capital markets (Craig, 2008). On the venture capital side, the dearth of initial public offerings, with only six companies going public in the USA in 2008, compared to an average of just less than fifty a year between 2001 and 2007, and over 180 a year between 1991 and 1998. With trade sales also hitting low points, the absence of proper exit paths severely hampered venture capitalists' ability to generate returns.

The recycler is not broken, so don't fix it!

Where does private equity go from here? No, the system is not broken. It has brought about the longest period of sustainable growth ever seen, and this across the broadest swath of geography. Private equity is doing just fine, and the current correction has just brought expectations in line with reality. What the world needs is more of it, not less. What private equity needs is less regulation, not more. This is money that has to come from mature, sophisticated, long-term investors with incentives to monitor their investments. No governmental entity will ever be able to provide the same quality of monitoring, in particular without the profit incentive. If investors were hurt this time, they largely have themselves to blame. The market has an uncanny ability ultimately to correct misbehaviour. But let us be clear that limiting or constraining private equity activities can lead only to one thing: less growth and ultimately less wealth for all. This is not what the economy needs today. What the economy needs is an acceptance of the critical role played by private equity in general in channelling money to the most creative and potent segments of the economy. Private equity is the ultimate rocket booster in the capitalistic system. You cannot ask a rocket booster to behave like an electric engine, but then again people would not have travelled to the moon without one....

References

Craig, Catherine (2008) 'Private Equity's Debt Buybacks Irk Bankers', *The Wall Street Journal Europe*, 10 September, p. 23.

Gompers, Paul and Lerner, Josh (2001) *The Money of Invention: How Venture Capital Creates New Wealth*, Harvard Business School Press.

Mawson, James (2009) 'Ten Largest Buyout Firms Can Spend $200 Billion', *The Wall Street Journal Europe*, 7 January, p. 25.

Meerkat, Hieno and Liechtenstein, Heinrich (2008) 'Get Ready for the Private Equity Shakeout', Working paper, The Boston Consulting Group (BCG), December.

Sudarsanam, Puliyur, Wright, Mike and Huang, Jian (2007) *Going Private Buyouts and Shareholder Wealth Gains: Impact of Bankruptcy Risk*, Working paper, Centre for Management Buy-out Research, Nottingham University.

Walker, Marcus, Ip, Greg and Batson, Andrew (2007) 'The High Cost of Growth – Inflation Fears Rise as Downward Pull on Prices Reverses', *The Wall Street Journal Europe*, 6 June.

7
A Concluding Reflection

Progress-driven business leaders, in synergy with their stakeholders, are engines of prosperity. This archetype of business leadership is likely to generate optimal benefits (material and non-material) for the wellbeing of individuals and humanity. The pinnacle of business achievements can be epitomized with attributes of genuine lasting value, capable of spreading globally and burgeoning into multifarious directions. An attempt is made here at identifying and classify major, albeit intertwined, factors conducive to the blossoming of business leadership for progress (see Exhibit 7.1).

1 *Geopolitical and geo-economic conditions.* These stand essentially for peace and socio-political stability; geography-geology; and demography. The latter's favourable conditions offer a potentially fertile basis for growth and progress, with peace constituting the absolute and primordial prerequisite.
2 *Resources.* These comprise human resources and accumulated know-how, material capital (financial and non-financial), natural resources, and others.
3 *Infrastructures.* These cover (a) basic physical facilities – such as those relating to water, energy, housing, telecommunications, transport and so on; and (b) socio-administrative institutions – notably those relating to learning, safety and security of people and property.
4 *Values and rights.* These are recognized by reference to universal norms. They include notably such components as the freedom of choice; fair and effective justice; accessible education; basic health and nutrition; and protection of culture, among others.

Exhibit 7.1 Pillars of progress

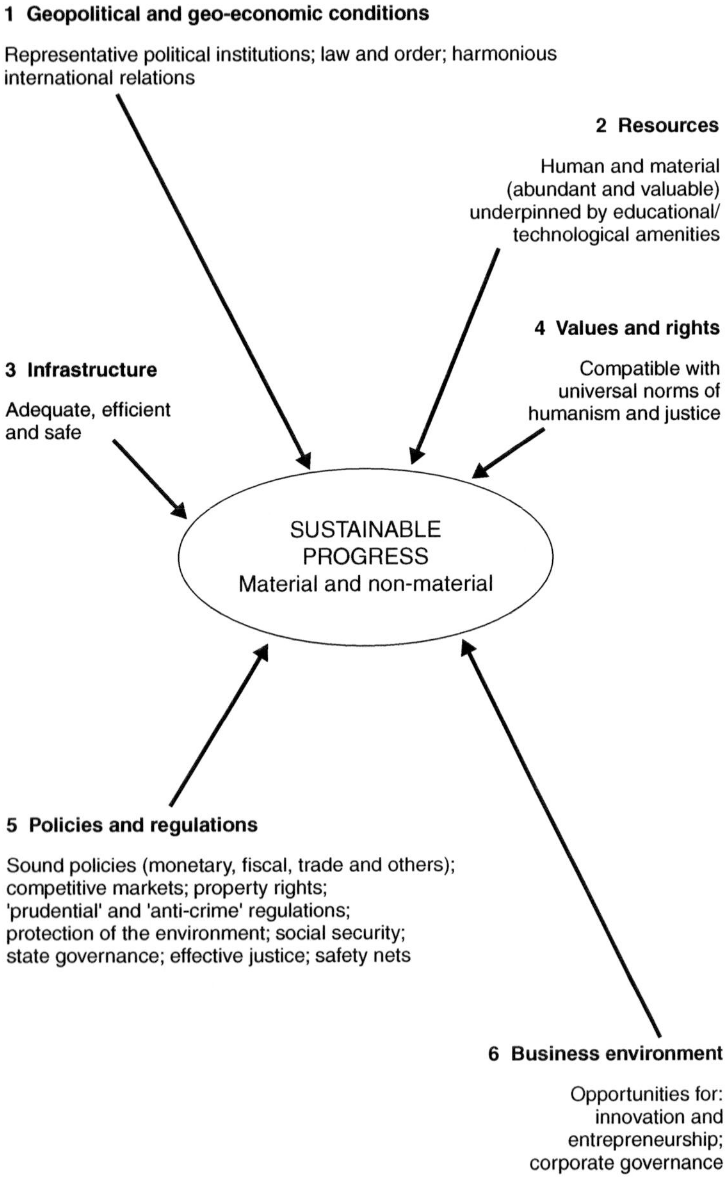

5 *Policies and regulations.* These concern, *inter alia,* public finance; exchange rates and flows of capital; employment, efficiency of markets and competitive behaviour; governance (transparency, accountability, and integrity of policies and practices); sound regulations and their vigilant enforcement.
6 *Business environment.* Multiple factors are involved, among which one could mention a social environment that favours risk-taking and a corpus of legislation that motivates inventors, innovators and entrepreneurs (with incentives and support).

The above-mentioned mainsprings of progress-driven entrepreneurial firms can be deemed valid for a large number of countries. Nevertheless, empirical case studies need to be carried out in order to understand the complex forces that influence the achievements (or conversely the failures) of individual enterprises or societies. Each of the above-mentioned six categories can be broken down into several components for detailed analysis and evaluation. Thus, state interventions need to be judged by reference to their soundness and effectiveness in attaining desired objectives – such as *sustainable progress* and *balanced sharing* in benefits and costs among stakeholders. Analysing 'state governance', the World Bank proposes six indicators: civil liberties and accountability; political stability and absence of violence; government effectiveness; regulatory quality; rule of law; and control of corruption among politicians, civil servants and businesses (see www.worldbank.org/wbi/governance/govdata). The data cover some 210 jurisdictions over an eight-year period and include subjective data such as 'perception of firms regarding government's interference in investment decisions'. Margins of errors in calculating these indicators exist, essentially owing to varying degrees of reliability of the sources used.

Among the principal drivers of progress, knowledge – catalyzed by entrepreneurial spirit – is reckoned to be the most important factor of production over the long term (see, for example, the periodical *OECD Review of Innovation Policy*; also Cotis, 2007 [available at: www.gemconsortium.org]; Rajan, 2006; Bergheim, 2008; Department for International Development, 2004; and Neuhaus, 2005 [available at: www.dbresearch.com]). To stoke up responsible entrepreneurial spirit, a sound and enforceable regulatory framework – based on honesty and accountability – is paramount. Accordingly, it is vital to eliminate the use of corporate assets for illegitimate personal gain, as was eloquently expressed by the chairman of the City of London's policy and resources committee thus: 'As the world's leading international centre of financial and business services (bigger in these terms than New York), London – and especially the City of London – risks being a honey-pot for white-collar criminals. It is a billion-dollar problem rooted in our trillion-dollar success' (see Snyder, 2006). This problem applies also to other financial centres. To protect against such a costly threat to London's reputation, the quoted regulator calls for the 'upgrading in the prevention, policing and punishment of fraud' (see also Transparency International; available at: www.transparency.org).

While one needs to caution against *excessive* governmental intervention or constraints that could thwart market efficiency and business dynamism, one should also warn against lack of vigilance or prudence on the part of regulators in exercising their watchdog function over markets and businesses under their responsibility. Their mission is to anticipate and contain malpractices or swindles through effective controls, before crises fester and contaminate whole sectors of national economies, eventually spreading internationally (see, for example, Collyns, 2008).

Some regulators and business quarters have argued dogmatically that mismanagement or excessive risks taken by individual firms and operators would be readily sanctioned by markets. Their hypothesis is that there is no need for exacting governmental regulations and unremitting controls, since dysfunctional situations and dereliction of duty are readily corrected by free market forces and/or self-regulation. Their claim is that the general loosening of governmental regulations and controls of markets and business entities would promote efficiency, growth and progress.

The above-mentioned hypothesis was espoused by Alan Greenspan, the chairman of the US Federal Reserve Board for eighteen and a half years until January 2006. It is revealing to note that, with the benefit of hindsight, he admitted *ex post* the limitations of his judgement, when he was in command at the inception of subprime mortgages in the USA (see Chapter 1). Responding to the questioning of the chairman of the Committee on Oversight and Government Reform, Representative Henry A. Waxman, Mr Greenspan said:

> I made a mistake in presuming that the self-interest of organizations, specifically banks and others, were such that they were best capable of protecting their own shareholders and their equity in the firms ... I found a flaw in the model that I perceived is the critical functioning structure that defines how the world works, so to speak' (*Hearings on the Financial Crisis and the role of Federal Regulators*, US House of Representatives, 23 October 2008, preliminary transcript).

Sound regulatory regimes are of vital importance to wealth creation and progress. It is therefore incumbent on the citizens' representatives to scrutinize continuously the adequacy of regulatory systems and regulators' judgement or practices. The crucial role of custodians of public interest is to exercise appropriate and timely controls over economic agents to contain unwarrantable risk-taking, deter violations and abuses, remedy market malfunctioning and quell simmering crises – quite a challenge in a world of complexity, continuous change, uncertainty and human frailty.

References

Bergheim, Stefan (2008) *Long-run Growth Forecasting* (Berlin/Heidelberg: Springer Verlag).

Collyns, Charles (2008) 'The Crisis through the Lens of History', *Finance & Development*, International Monetary Fund, December, pp. 18–20.

Cotis, Jean-Philippe, OECD Chief Economist (2007) 'Entrepreneurship as an Engine for Growth: Evidence and Policy Challenges', GEM Forum on Entrepreneurship: Setting the Development Agenda, London, 10 and 11 January.

Department for International Development (2004) *The Importance of Financial Sector Development for Growth and Poverty Reduction*, London, August.

IMF (International Monetary Fund) (2005) 'Why Measuring Governance Matters', IMF survey, Washington, DC, 1 August, pp. 230–1.

Neuhaus, Marco (2005) *Opening Economies Succeed – More Trade Boosts Growth*, (Frankfurt am Main: Deutsche Bank Research), 11 November.

Rajan, Raghuram (2006) 'From Paternalistic to Enabling', *Finance & Development*, September, pp. 54–6.

Snyder, Michael (2006) 'Fraud Is Threatening the Global Reputation of the City', *Financial Times*, 31 July, p. 15.

World Bank, The (2004) *A Better Investment Climate for Everyone – World Development Report 2005* (Washington, DC: The World Bank).

Index